t.f.h.

ALL (87) BREED DOG GROOMING
for the beginner

TS-101

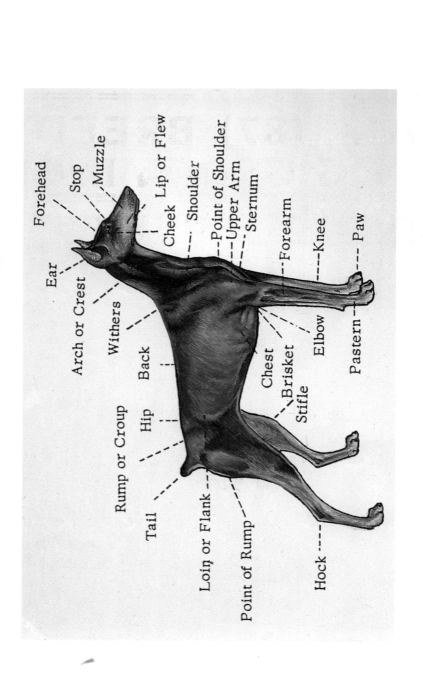

t.f.h.

ALL (87) BREED
DOG GROOMING
for the beginner

Photos by Isabelle Francais.

Distributed in the UNITED STATES by T.F.H. Publications, Inc., One T.F.H. Plaza, Neptune City, NJ 07753; in CANADA to the Pet Trade by H & L Pet Supplies Inc., 27 Kingston Crescent, Kitchener, Ontario N2B 2T6; Rolf C. Hagen Ltd., 3225 Sartelon Street, Montreal 382 Quebec; in CANADA to the Book Trade by Macmillan of Canada (A Division of Canada Publishing Corporation), 164 Commander Boulevard, Agincourt, Ontario M1S 3C7; in ENGLAND by T.F.H. Publications Limited, 4 Kier Park, Ascot, Berkshire SL5 7DS; in AUSTRALIA AND THE SOUTH PACIFIC by T.F.H. (Australia) Pty. Ltd., Box 149, Brookvale 2100 N.S.W., Australia; in NEW ZEALAND by Ross Haines & Son, Ltd., 18 Monmouth Street, Grey Lynn, Auckland 2, New Zealand; in SINGAPORE AND MALAYSIA by MPH Distributors (S) Pte., Ltd., 601 Sims Drive, #03/07/21, Singapore 1438; in the PHILIPPINES by Bio-Research, 5 Lippay Street, San Lorenzo Village, Makati Rizal; in SOUTH AFRICA by Multipet Pty. Ltd., 30 Turners Avenue, Durban 4001. Published by T.F.H. Publications, Inc. Manufactured in the United States of America by T.F.H. Publications, Inc.

CONTENTS

THE CONTRIBUTORS 8
GENERAL INFORMATION 11

Affenpinscher, 49
Afghan Hound, 51
Airedale Terrier, 52
Akita, 55
Alaskan Malamute, 57
Australian Terrier, 58
Basset Hound, 60
Beagle, 62
Bearded Collie, 63
Bedlington Terrier, 65
Border Terrier, 68
Borzoi, 70
Boston Terrier, 71
Bouvier des Flandres, 72
Boxer, 75
Brittany Spaniel, 76
Bulldog, 78
Cardigan Welsh Corgi, 79
Chesapeake Bay Retriever, 81
Chihuahua, long coat, 82
Chihuahua, smooth coat, 83
Chow Chow, 84
Cocker Spaniel, American, 86
Cocker Spaniel, English, 88
Collie, rough coat, 90
Collie, smooth coat, 92
Dachshund, long coat, 94
Dachshund, smooth coat, 95
Dachshund, wire coat, 96

Dalmatian, 97
Doberman Pinscher, 98
English Setter, 99
English Springer Spaniel, 101
Flat-coated Retriever, 103
Fox Terrier, smooth, 105
Fox Terrier, wire, 106
French Bulldog, 109
German Shepherd Dog, 110
German Shorthaired Pointer, 111
German Wirehaired Pointer, 112
Golden Retriever, 114
Great Dane, 115
Greyhound, 116
Irish Setter, 118
Italian Greyhound, 121
Keeshond, 122
Kerry Blue Terrier, 124
Labrador Retriever, 127
Lhasa Apso, 128
Maltese, 130
Miniature Schnauzer, 132
Newfoundland, 134
Norwegian Elkhound, 135
Old English Sheepdog, 137
Pekingese, 138
Pembroke Welsh Corgi, 140
Pointer, 141

Pomeranian, 142
Poodle (Dutch clip), 146
Poodle (Kennel clip), 144
Poodle (Lamb clip), 149
Poodle (Puppy clip), 151
Poodle (Royal Dutch clip), 153
Poodle (Summer clip), 155
Poodle (Town and Country clip), 157
Poodle Heads and Faces, Clean face, 159
Poodle Heads and Faces, Moustache, 160
Pug, 162
Rottweiler, 164
Samoyed, 165
Scottish Terrier, 166
Sealyham Terrier, 169
Shetland Sheepdog, 171
Shih Tzu, 173
Siberian Husky, 175
Silky Terrier, 176
Skye Terrier, 177
Staffordshire Bull, 179
Standard Schnauzer, 180
Vizsla, 183
Weimaraner, 184
Welsh Terrier, 185
West Highland White Terrier, 188
Yorkshire Terrier, 190

INDEX 192

THE CONTRIBUTORS

Richard Davis, Illustrator

Richard Davis received his Masters Degree in Fine Arts from Mason Gross School of the Arts, New Brunswick, New Jersey, and his Bachelor of Fine Arts from Monmouth College, West Long Branch, New Jersey. He divides his time between painting, freelance illustrating, and being employed as an adjunct art instructor at Ocean County College, Toms River, New Jersey.

Richard's work has been widely exhibited throughout New Jersey, including group shows at The State Museum, Trenton. Outside New Jersey, he has participated in shows on Long Island and in New York

Gay M. Ernst

Gay M. Ernst has been involved in grooming, breeding, and showing dogs since 1955. With the purchase of a show-quality Cocker Spaniel that year, and the apprenticeship to the proprietor of a grooming shop in Manhattan, she became totally immersed in the dog world.

In 1961 she married William Ernst, who became a top handler of show Cockers. Together they owned and operated the Dapper Dog Den in Manhattan from 1961 to 1969. Bill Ernst and Gay combined names to establish BeGay Cockers and bought a kennel in New Milford, Connecticut, which they had from 1966 to 1977.

The untimely death of Bill in 1977 brought about the closing of the kennel, and Gay moved to East Hampton, New York, with the couple's three children and the Cocker Spaniels. In 1978 she established a grooming shop in nearby Bridgehampton and continued to breed Cockers under the BeGay prefix. To date there are over 50 BeGay champion Cocker Spaniels, including many record-breaking dogs of unusual colors.

Susan Gutman

Susan Gutman is the owner of Dog Patch, an all-breed grooming shop in Westfield, New Jersey. A graduate of the New York School of Dog Grooming, she has been working in the field of grooming since

1974. Her shop, which employs nine people, has offered its services to local fund-raising organizations, such as the American Heart Association, for which she has sponsored a yearly groom-a-thon.

Susan has lectured to the Union County 4-H dog club and the seeing-eye club on routine home pet care and has opened her shop to local scout groups who are studying pet care in order to achieve their merit badges.

In 1986, Susan was the first guest on the Storer Cable Communications network's pet program, speaking on the topic of summer pet care.

Sandy King

Sandy King has been in business as a dog groomer since 1965 and has taught dog grooming since 1970. Besides grooming, she has been active in other aspects of the dog fancy as well: namely, in the showing of Siberian Huskies, Doberman Pinschers, and German Shepherd Dogs; and as a writer of a dog column for the *Easton Express* for twelve years. Sandy is a member of the National Dog Groomers Association and is the Pennsylvania coordinator for PIJAC, the Pet Industry Joint Advisory Council.

Gloria Lewis

Gloria Lewis has been a breeder of champion Miniature Schnauzers for 25 years. She is a professional groomer and show handler of this breed, as well as co-author with Beverly Pisano of *Miniatures Schnauzers,* published by T.F.H. Many of her show dogs are featured in Anna Katherine Nicholas's *The Book of the Miniature Schnauzer* (another T.F.H. book), and they have also been featured on AKC *Gazette* covers.

Susan Tapp

Susan Tapp has been involved with dogs for over 15 years, having obtained obedience titles and breed championships on many of them. She is a certified master groomer (C.M.G.) by the Professional Pet Groomers Certification, Inc. (P.P.G.C.) and has won several grooming contests to date. Susan was an instructor at a large, accredited grooming school for some time, and currently she gives private lessons. She is involved with local grooming associations and kennel clubs and is very active in showing her Irish Water Spaniels in obedience, breed, and grooming contests. With such a busy schedule, she still finds time to run her own grooming salon, Canine Castle.

Pat Wehrle

Pat Wehrle is a dog groomer and freelance artist. She has exhibited Pugs for five years and has owned them for seventeen. In 1983 Pat was Category Winner in the Pug Dog Club of Greater New York Photo Contest, taking the Grand Prize in 1984.

Chelsea Youngblood-Killeen

Chelsea Youngblood-Killeen started grooming a few years ago, back home in England. She and her family lived in a small town, Woodstock, on the outskirts of Oxford, and her parents owned two miniature Poodles. Chelsea was always interested in how these dogs were groomed and one time when they were due to be clipped, she took her mother's dressmaking scissors and did a wonderful chop-up job on both of them! The initial shock to her parents was dismay, which gradually changed to humor, and eventually to wild laughter. However, they decided that if that was what she wanted to do, then she could practice on their dogs. This she did religiously, for weeks, until she could scissor both dogs into cute fluff balls, which she now did with the help of a metal comb and professional scissors purchased by her mother.

At that time, Anne, the wife of the local pet shop owner, decided to "retire" from grooming dogs and become a full-time mother and housewife. Geoff, her husband, then asked Chelsea if she would be interested in learning how to groom dogs. She was ecstatic and said she could start the next day! Armed with her comb, scissors, and an acquired brush, she rushed over bright and early. Geoff gave her a Poodle, a clipper, and blades and told her to groom the dog. It took about three hours from start to finish and Chelsea had no problem with the scissoring, as she had practiced for so many weeks at home.

From then on it became easier with Geoff's and Anne's guidance, and improvement came with every dog she clipped. She stayed with the shop for about three years, learning a great deal about dogs and clips from numerous visits to the Crufts Dog Show.

Over the years Chelsea has groomed dogs in Germany, where she lived for a while and learned the Van Büren Poodle Clip. This consists of not shaving anything, except the belly and rear areas, and scissoring the whole dog evenly (which reminded her of her formative years in grooming).

In the United States Chelsea first lived in South Carolina, working in a grooming shop where the owner owned and showed five Bichon Frises. This woman taught her how to groom Bichons for show and in accordance with what judges would be looking for.

10

GENERAL INFORMATION

Dematting

Spray the coat with a detangling lotion, ensuring that you saturate all tangled areas. Let the dog sit for 5 or 10 minutes before you start working on his coat. Using a slicker brush and a matting comb and starting at the bottom of his legs, work in very small sections at a time, taking the coat in layers. Brush the coat up and then down to loosen the mats, alternating with a matting comb. It is important that all mats be combed out before the bath, as shampoo gets caught in them and is hard to rinse out. Water tends to tighten a mat, and drying shrinks it into a tighter knot. So you can see what a mess you'll have if you fail to comb out mats prior to bathing.

Dematting should never to torturous for the dog. Dogs have different degrees of tolerance: some dogs do not seem to mind the tugging and pulling involved, while other dogs get extremely upset with just the slightest degree of pulling. Dematting should *never* cause a dog severe stress. If the dog does not accept dematting, or if it is impossible to remove the mats, the groomer should get permission from the owner to shave the coat down with a #10 or #7 blade. When the new coat comes in, the dog should be groomed on a regular basis so it does not get severely matted again. Dogs that do not tolerate combing easily should be groomed on a 3 to 4 week schedule or sooner.

There are all sorts of shampoos available, depending on the type of coat you are working on. Be sure to remove all mats and tangles prior to bathing; otherwise, the shampoo will get caught in them and will be hard to get out.

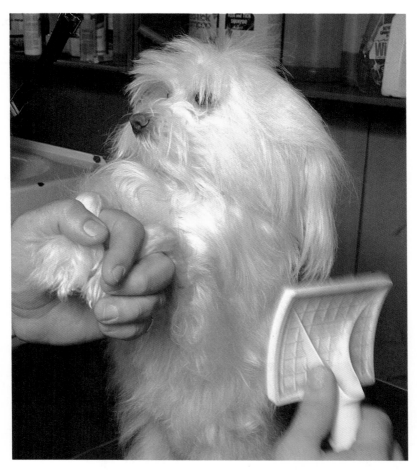

Brush out all loose and dead hair from the coat before bathing the dog. The more hair you remove now, the less you have to deal with later.

Bathing

A good bath is all important to a good grooming. You can not finish a dog well if he is not clean. In order to thoroughly clean the dog, you must be sure to lather well to remove all dirt and rinse well to remove all soap. Shampoos available today do not strip oil from a dog's coat, rather they add to the coat. A good bath makes your dog feel better, look better, and definitely smell better.

Be sure to brush the dog's coat before the bath. Brushing removes dead hair and debris, separates the hair, and stimulates circulation. All mats and tangles should be combed out (see Dematting section) prior to bathing a dog.

Properly securing you dog in the tub will keep him safe and prevent you from getting soaked. The use of a nylon leash and collar helps keep a dog still while you bathe him. If your dog is cooperative, you'll need only one hook in the wall, about middle of the tub, to tie him to. For dogs that are more active, or for large breeds, it's good to have three hooks on the back wall behind the tub—one at the front for his head, one in the middle, and one at the back end of the dog. The dog's head can be hooked to the front and middle hooks if necessary, and a belly band can be put on the dog and hooked to the back. To prevent yourself from getting soaked, be sure the dog's head does not extend over the edge of the tub. Hooking the dog in this way makes him feel secure and it prevents him from turning around or sitting down during the bath.

Be sure to use a rubber mat in the tub. It is also recommended that you use nylon leashes and nylon collars to secure the dog in the tub. If a dog should ever become upset or start thrashing around and you need to get him loose quickly, you can always cut him loose if you use nylon instead of metal choke chains.

Getting a small dog into the tub is no problem. A 90 pound bruiser is another story! The most comfortable tubs for dog groomers are waist high, so you need to work at training large dogs to be

Place a rubber mat in the bottom of the tub to keep the dog from slipping.

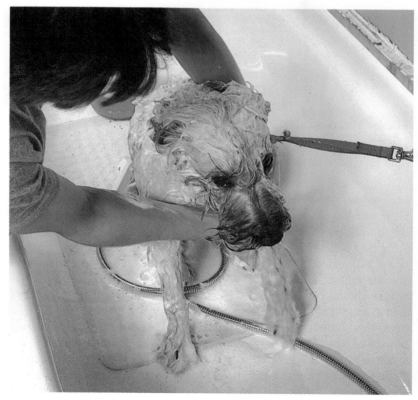

through the hair to the skin. Be sure to do the entire dog—under the stomach, under the tail, under and between the foot pads, inside the ear leather. Do not get shampoo in the dog's eyes: tearless shampoos may not sting, but any type of shampoo (and dirt) can cause eye infection. If certain areas are extremely dirty, such as the legs or feet, use a small bristle brush to gently scrub these areas.

When the dog's coat is well lathered, rinse with warm water, using a spray with a good force of water. Rinse the head back from the eyes so soap does not run into them, and protect the ear canal with your thumb, being careful not to direct spray into it. Rinse around one ear first, then do the other. If a dog is extremely dirty, relather the entire dog again. Rinse until all traces of soap are removed from the coat.

Squeeze the water out of the coat with your hands or use a high velocity dryer to blow water off the dog while he is still in the tub. Wrap the dog in a large towel and take him out of the tub, placing him on a grooming table covered with a heavy bath mat. Towel dry the dog on the mat, which helps absorb water from the feet and speeds up drying time.

A thorough rinsing is especially important, to ensure that all traces of shampoo are removed from the dog's coat. A hose with a spray attachment works well for this purpose.

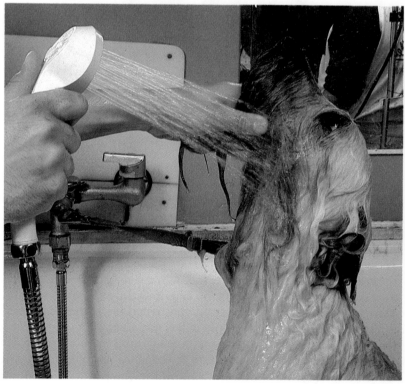

No matter what drying method you select—cage drying or drying on the grooming table with a hand-held dryer—first give the dog a good rub-down with a large, absorbent towel. This removes excess water from the coat.

Cleaning the Ears

Remove ear dirt and wax by swabbing the ears with a cotton ball moistened with ear cleaner. Then dry out each ear with a dry cotton ball and dust the ear with a medicated ear powder. The ear powder makes it easier to pull hair out of the ear and also helps prevent ear infection.

With some breeds, there is more accumulation of hair at the entrance to the ear canal than with other breeds, so it must be removed. Ear hair may be pulled out with the fingers or with ear forceps. If you use your fingers, be sure to wash your hands well between dogs, as ear mites can be transmitted under the fingernails. When you pull ear hair, take hold of the dog's ear, lift it up, and lay it flat on his head. This allows you to pull hair from the external ear but closes off the inner ear and protects it. Pull small bits of hair at a time in order to make it more comfortable for the dog.

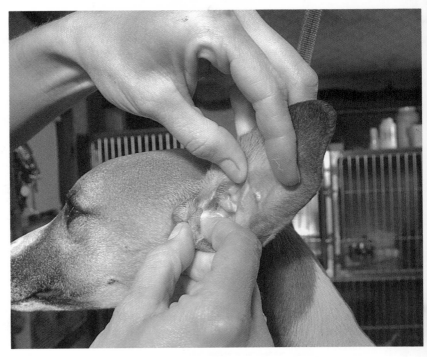

Cleaning the ears (top) should be part of every grooming session, regardless of what breed you are working on. Accumulated dirt and wax must be removed gently. The eyes (bottom) should also be checked, and wiped clean if necessary.

Cleaning the Eyes

Eye cleaning should not be overlooked as a part of grooming. The frequency of eye cleaning care varies according to the breed of dog. A dog with protuberant eyes, such as the Bulldog, should have its eyes cleaned regularly.

A veterinarian should be consulted if the eyes are red or tender. He or she can also recommend preparations which can be used to clean stains caused by normal eye secretions.

Cleaning Facial Wrinkles

In a dog such as the Shar-Pei, and others, special attention must be given to facial wrinkles. Keeping the wrinkles dirt-free and dry will ward off irritation and infection.

Facial wrinkles should first be cleansed with *warm* water and then gently dried. If signs of redness are present, apply a light dusting of corn starch, baby powder, or talcum powder. Facial wrinkles should be cleaned weekly.

The Chinese Shar-pei, with his many wrinkles, needs special attention. After bathing him, make certain that each fold of skin is clean and dry. Any dampness that remains is sure to cause infection.

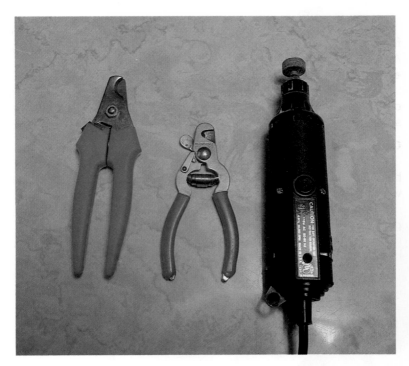

For dogs whose nails do not wear down naturally as a result of exercising on abrasive surfaces, such as asphalt, nail care becomes extremely important. Nail clippers and nail groomers (which grind smooth the clipped nail) are indispensable grooming tools.

Nail Clipping

Dogs that regularly exercise or play outdoors on abrasive surfaces will generally require less frequent nail clipping than those kept mainly in the house or on soft ground.

When clipping a dog's nails, one must be careful not to cut the "quick," a blood vessel in the nail. Cutting the quick will cause the dog pain and may result in future "battles" when a manicure is needed. Keep styptic power (or a styptic pencil) handy in case of an emergency.

Holding the dog's paw carefully, snip off just the very tip of each nail. Ragged nail surfaces may be smoothed away by using a file.

Note: Although the correct terminology for *nail,* as applied to dogs, is *claw,* nail is used throughout the text as it is the favored word in the grooming trade.

Conditioning the Coat

Keeping a dog's coat in condition may be compared with keeping your own hair in condition. Just as human hair care specialists offer special oil treatments, massages, and chemicals, so are there similar products available for conditioning the coat of a dog.

The edges of the nails may be rough after clipping them. If this is the case, smooth them with a nail groomer.

In almost all cases, simple brushing will keep dog coats in excellent condition. Dogs need oil in their coats to maintain their essential waterproofing. If your dog's coat is dry it means that its diet is probably lacking in fats.

There are many products on the market that can be called "in general" coat conditioners. Try some, as each seems to be good for certain types of dogs' coats and poor for others.

Dry Cleaning Dog Coats

The dog has just been groomed and runs under a parked car and gets oil or grease on its back. What to do? The answer is simple. Use a dry cleaning agent. You have a puppy that is too young to be bathed. It gets itself dirty. How do you clean it? Use a dry cleaner.

Basically a "dry cleaner" may or may not be "dry." There are foams and sprays that should be considered as "spot removers." You can use these foams on a whole dog if you wish, but it's a lot of work. There are dry cleaning powders, too. None works as well as a good bath if you must do a whole dog. All, however, work pretty well for removing small areas, especially on white dogs.

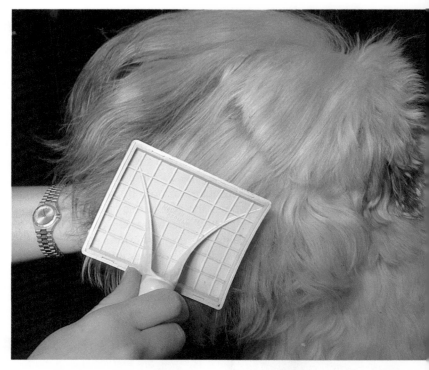

A curved slicker brush (top) works well on longhaired breeds. To make the coat of this dog (bottom) full and fluffy, the groomer brushes out the coat as it is being dried with warm air from the hair dryer.

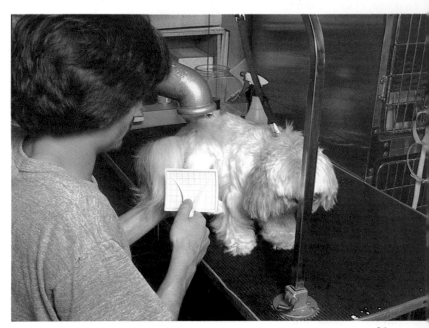

Experience will dictate which type of dry cleaner to use in a given situation. *One word of caution:* All dry cleaners have a chemical basis to them. They may cause skin problems for sensitive dogs, and they may cause serious matting in long-haired breeds. Use care.

Forced Drying

Just as in your own case, you can dry your hair in the air, use a series of dry towels and rub vigorously, or use an electric hair dryer that blasts your hair with hot air. The same techniques are available for dogs. All professionals must have their own forced hot air dryers. In this manner the dog's hair, like a human's hair, can be blow-dried, making it fluffier and more professional looking.

Blow-drying as a technique requires using a brush to fluff the coat as you dry it. The brush entangles the hair and is twisted so as to expose the roots. The hot air is then directed against the brush (it would be too hot to direct against the dog's skin). As soon as the hair on the brush is dried, the blower is moved away and the hair is brushed to fluffiness. This is repeated over and over again until the entire dog is dried. Obviously this technique cannot be used on short-

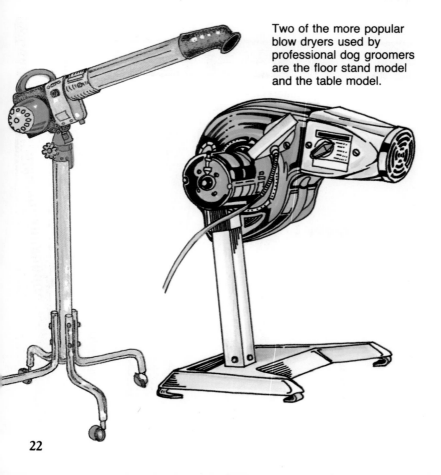

Two of the more popular blow dryers used by professional dog groomers are the floor stand model and the table model.

haired breeds! Success in using it with certain breeds, like Poodles, requires greater skill than with other breeds, since the fluffed shape of the head and body is important to the general appearance of the dog.

Cage drying is merely attaching a dryer to a cage so that the heated dry air constantly bathes the dog, drying its hair. This is a technique used mainly with short-haired breeds or breeds whose coats do not need fluffing (like Irish Setters). Special drying cages are available. They have lots of ventilation.

Towel or air drying is merely to allow the dog to shake itself free of the loose water in its coat. Then briskly rub the dog all over using dry towels. Finally, though the dog is still damp, it is released. The hair dries normally or, more usually, the dog rolls around on the grass or on your carpet to hasten the drying process.

Air drying and towel drying are acceptable in the summer. But when it is cold outside, the dog should not be allowed freedom until its coat is thoroughly dried.

For shorthaired breeds or those that do not have to be fluff dried, cage drying is the solution.

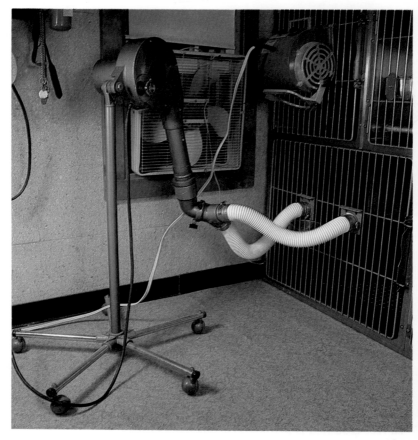

Hoses have been attached to a floor dryer and then fastened to the side of the cage in which this Cardigan Welsh Corgi relaxes.

Grooming a Dog's Feet

Long-haired breeds are highly inbred strains. They are abnormal when compared to the wild dogs, wolves, and dog-like descendants from which we assume dogs have originated. Thus the long hair on the body includes abnormally long hair on the feet. The hair growing between the pads of the feet must be removed in all long-haired breeds except the Poodle and certain long-haired breeds that spend a lot of time walking on ice or snow. A clue to a dog's need to have its feet groomed is that it constantly chews on its feet.

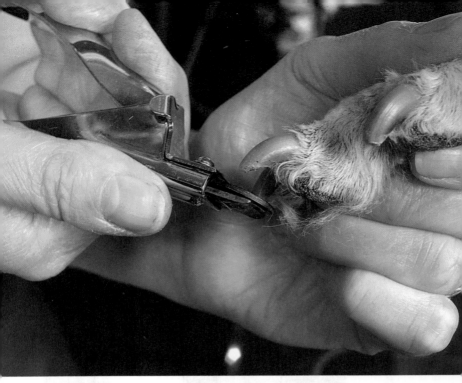

When clipping the nails (top), use a nail clipper made specifically for dogs. For most every dog breed, the hair between the foot pads will have to be clipped (bottom).

Using a small scissors or your clipper with a suitable fine blade (#10 or #15), clip the hair on the feet between the pads uncleanly. Leave a stubble, as this protects the delicate skin between the pads, especially in the winter. Many dogs want to jump into their master's arms when they have to walk on ice because their feet are so cold!

Grooming The Underside

At the same time you are grooming the dog's feet, you can groom its stomach and anal areas. The same tools are required ... scissors and/or a clipper with a #10 blade.

The stomach on most dogs should be shaved close but not absolutely clean. Male dogs should have the hair on their penis cropped closely, too, so it doesn't pick up dirt.

The anal pore should be clipped clean, and the hair on long-haired breeds should be cropped in the anal area so the hair doesn't pick up debris as the dog excretes. DO NOT ACTUALLY USE A CLIPPER ON THE ANAL MUSCLE, UPON WHICH NO HAIR GROWS. This is a sensitive area and will make your dog uncomfortable, perhaps even causing an infection.

A scissors is, perhaps, the best tool for the job of removing hair around the anal pore, since it doesn't have actual contact with the skin and will remove enough of the longer hairs to do the job.

The loop, fastened securely but not tightly around the Italian Greyhound's neck, helps to keep the dog still while the groomer clips stray hairs from his underside.

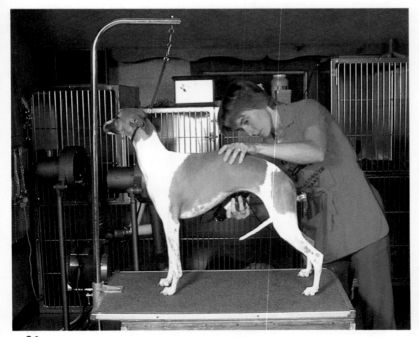

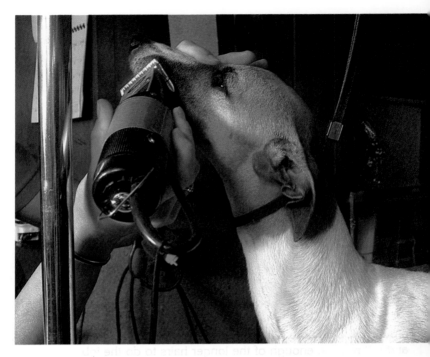

Some professionals snip the whiskers from a dog's muzzle, using blunt-tip scissors; others, however, prefer to clip them with an electric clipper.

Removing the Whiskers

Show groomers pay special attention to the facial hairs. Pet owners, however, have different tastes as far as whiskers are concerned. If the hairs are to be removed, use the same tools as above, namely a scissors or a clipper with a #10 or #15 blade. Many dogs, especially Poodles, have the shape of their faces determined by grooming. Thus it is up to the individual owners as to how they like their dogs to look.

Doggie Odors and Colognes

Every dog has two glands alongside his anal pore; these glands must be emptied. Nature usually takes care of this when the dog defecates. Sometimes, though, they become clogged and enlarge, making them uncomfortable for the dog. It is not a dog groomer's responsibility to empty these glands, even though it is relatively easy. This is a job for a veterinarian. There may be serious underlying reasons why the glands are not emptying themselves, and the vet should be consulted. If that area of a dog has a bad odor, you should have it checked by a veterinarian anyway.

Using colognes and/or deodorizers is a matter of choice. There are many owners who use expensive perfumes on their dogs because they carry them and don't want their dog's cologne to conflict with their own.

Plucking and Stripping

In days long gone by, plucking wire-haired breeds was considered the way to go. This painful technique should be used only when the dog is shedding normally. Using your thumb and index finger, you grasp a small group of hair and quickly jerk it out. It hurts just to think about it . . . but that's all that plucking is. The way you pluck your own eyebrows (if you do!). It hurts. Show ring groomers use plucking with certain wire-haired breeds (schnauzers and terriers). It is not recommended.

Stripping is like plucking, but you use your thumb against a stripping knife blade and cut as you tear. This is a technique which was considered more humane than a plucking job, but it is far too trying for the groomer—to say nothing about the dog! Thinning shears serve the purpose almost as well . . . as does normal clipping.

Shedding

Most dogs shed naturally. With long-haired breeds, such as the Old English Sheepdog, a thorough brushing about three times a week will prevent matting and help maintain the overall appearance of the coat.

A small pin brush is used to remove loose hair and to break up the coat of this Pomeranian. Brushing is vitally important for this breed, in order to achieve the desired "powder puff" look.

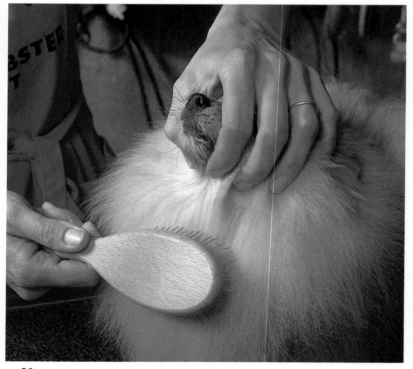

Many dogs are accustomed to being brushed by their owners, and these dogs truly are a pleasure to groom! Dogs that are difficult to control, however, must be held steadily with one hand while being brushed with the other.

Care of Pasterns and Leg Joints

Some large breeds, such as the St. Bernard and the German Shorthaired Pointer, require special attention to their pasterns and leg joints (hocks and elbows). Irritation and bald spots, caused by the dog's lying on abrasive surfaces, may occur. For prevention or relief, use a preparation recommended by your veterinarian.

Handling During Grooming

Accustoming your dog to grooming at an early age will—in the long run—make it an easier job for you.

Firmness and patience on your part, along with a calm environment, are important requirements. Establish that you are in control at the very start of the grooming procedure. Give the dog commands in a *kind,* yet *firm,* manner. During the grooming session, praise him when he obeys your commands. Never try to rush through a grooming routine.

Brush Burns

Brush burns, the result of excessive force when brushing during dematting, are a sign of carelessness on the part of the groomer. Brush burns result when the wire bristles of the slicker brush abrade the dog's skin. For brush burn treatment, your veterinarian can prescribe an unguent that will soothe and heal the injured areas.

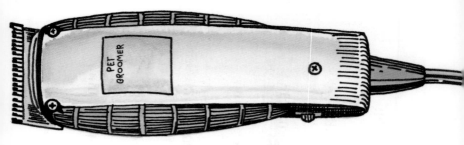

Electric clippers are manufactured with interchangeable blades, which vary according to coat type and length desired.

Clipping

The basis of modern dog grooming is the clipper, which has different blades. Just as, in the old days, hair was cut only with scissors, now human hair-cutting (especially for men's short hair) is done with a clipper. The idea in using a clipper is to gently cut away excess hair, leaving hair in a desired, predetermined length. The clipper is not an electric razor, which removes all of the hair.

Flexibility of the wrist is important whenever you are clipping a dog. By following this simple guideline, you will avoid clipper nicks as well as mistakes in coat styling.

Work carefully. Keep the blade flat against the section being clipped, and always move the clipper in the direction of the grain of the hair, unless grooming instructions specify another method.

DO NOT DIG INTO THE SKIN WITH A CLIPPER. It produces burns and cuts. Learning how to use a clipper is easy, but it is an art that *must* be mastered.

The same is true of scissoring. After the clipping, scissors are used to put on the finishing touches. How you use a pair of scissors is a measure of your skill. In any case, the scissors must be very sharp at all times or they'll pull the hair and perhaps earn you a dog bite!

Clipping and scissoring are what dog grooming is all about. If you can't handle these two techniques, let someone else do it, for you will never make a dog groomer.

Equipment

- *Pure boar bristle brush* — Excellent for regular brushing. Removes loose hair and distributes dog's natural oil from the skin down the hair shaft. Promotes healthy, shiny coat.
- *Slicker brush* — Wire pin brush with a hook pin that helps break up mats.
- *Curved slicker brush* — Curved slicker brush with heavier pins. Works extremely well on heavily longcoated dogs, such as the Old English Sheepdog.

30

There are all sorts of brushes available, depending on the specific grooming need. Generally speaking, a bristle brush (top) is good for brushing the coat of shorthaired breeds, while a slicker brush (bottom) is used to brush and de-matt the coat of longhaired breeds.

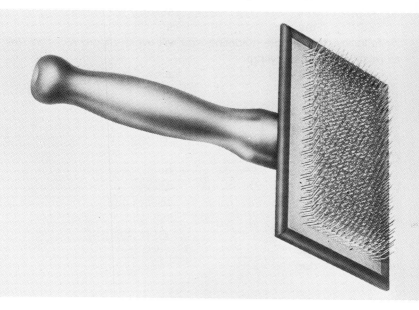

- *Ever gentle slicker* — Fine wire pin brush, lighter in weight, to be used on Poodles and matted toy dogs such as Yorkshire Terriers.
- *Pin brush* — Comes in many sizes and shapes from small, used on toy dogs, to large, used on Collies, etc. Excellent for breaking up the coat and removing loose hair. Pins must be good quality and retain their shape.
- *Rubber brush* — One of the finest brushes for removing dust and loose hair on shorthaired breeds. Also works well on cats.

31

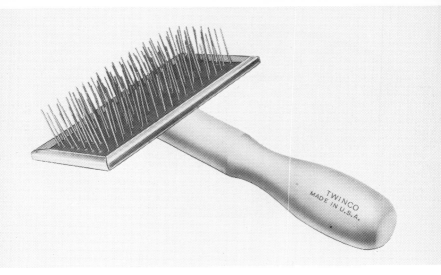

Slicker brushes (top and bottom) come in various sizes. Prior to bathing, these brushes are used to remove matts and tangles in the coat. A dog that is bathed without being brushed first is almost impossible to work on. Not only will it be difficult for you to groom him, but it will be uncomfortable for the dog.

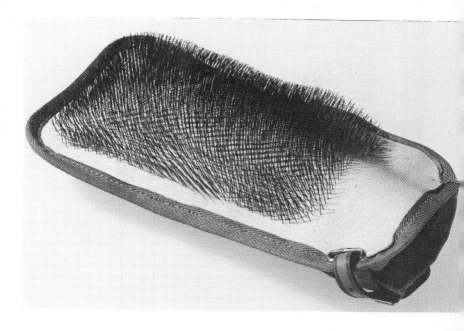

The hound glove (top) is great for brushing a short, smooth coat, like that of the Beagle or the Bloodhound. Before grooming a dog, have all of the necessary equipment at hand (bottom).

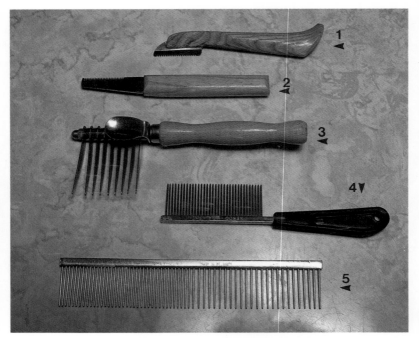

Fine and coarse stripping knives (1 and 2) are used primarily on harsh terrier coats. The wide-toothed matt comb (3) is useful whenever you have to remove tangles and matts from a dog with long hair. This medium-toothed comb (4) is designed for general work. The most versatile comb is the fine–medium combination (5).

- *Rubber curry brush* — Takes out dust and dirt on shorthaired breeds.
- *Hound glove* — Polishes and shines short coats, such as those of Doberman Pinschers and Basset Hounds.
- *Chamois cloth* — Used to polish and shine the coats of shorthaired dogs.
- *Combs* — Combs come in many shapes and styles. The most commonly used comb is the fine-medium combination. It is important that the comb is comfortable in your hand and that the teeth are properly spaced for the particular coat you are working on.
- *Mat comb* — Mat combs are designed to cut through mats without destroying the coat. They have a heavier tooth, are sharp on one side, and can be resharpened. Left-handed groomers can use these combs with ease as they're reversible. Some mat combs have one tooth only and have replaceable razor blades in them. Mat combs must be kept in good condition.
- *Molting comb* — These come in two styles, one for shorthaired breeds and one for longhaired breeds. They do an excellent job of removing loose undercoat.
- *Wood utility comb* — Excellent for getting through really long

coats, like that of the Collie. Easy on the hand, it is excellent for combing deep into a heavy coat and pulling out loose undercoats.

- *Undercoat rake* — Excellent to loosen up the coat and remove dead undercoat. Especially good on breeds like the German Shepherd Dog.
- *Shed'n blade* — Removes loose hair only. Pulls out loose top coat and undercoat.
- *Small Shed'n blade* — Takes out loose top coat and undercoat. Good for small dogs, like Chihuahuas, and shorthaired cats.
- *Duplex dresser* — Stripping knife with a removable razor blade.
- *Stripping knife* — Comes in fine, medium, and coarse styles. Generally, fine is used on the head, ears, and areas where hair is fine and delicate. Medium and coarse blades are usually used on the body.
- *Scissors* — These come in various sizes from tiny ear and nose scissors to long, straight grooming shears. Scissors must be well balanced and comfortable to use, and they should hold an edge well. Select ones that can be resharpened. Since everyone has a personal preference for a particular style of scissor, select yours with care.

Thinning shears (1 and 2) work well on dogs that have feathering, such as the Irish Setter or the American Cocker Spaniel. Ear forceps (3) enable you to gently pluck stray hair from the ears. Shears come in various sizes: small (4) for detail work, large (5) for heavily-coated breeds, and medium (6) for general scissoring.

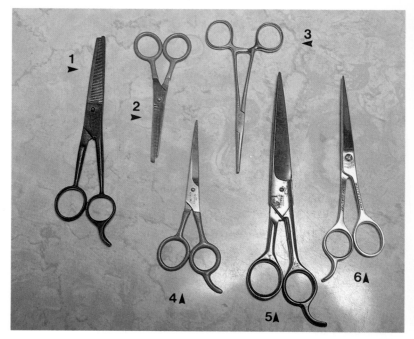

- *Thinning shears* — The type of thinning shear you use depends on the type of coat you are working on. Styles include those with a double or single edge, 30-46 teeth.

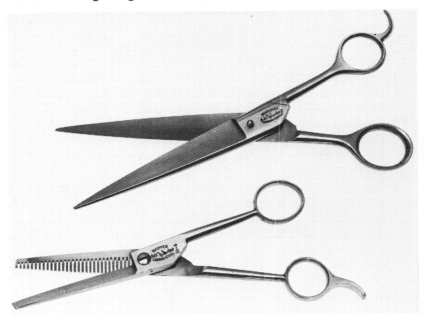

Most scissors (shears) are made with a single finger rest for ease of handling. Since scissoring is an art and can be quite strenuous, you will need to select scissors that are comfortable and easy to use.

- *Ear forceps* — Come in various sizes and weights. Some are curved; others are straight. A groomer's preference determines which is most comfortable to use.
- *Nail clipper* (guillotine style) — Comes in a regular size for most medium-sized dogs and an extra-large size for larger breeds. The scissor-style clipper is recommended for small dogs and cats. The extra-large scissor-style clipper is excellent for dewclaws that grow excessively long.
- *Grooming table* — Standard grooming tables are 24" x 36"; however, there are smaller tables which measure 18" x 24". If you are not doing large dogs, use the smaller table. Some dogs behave better if they do not have a lot of room to dance around on. All tables should have a top made of rubber or some other non-skid material that is easy to disinfect.
- *Hydraulic tables* — Come in various sizes and shapes. They can be raised, lowered, and turned in a full circle. Although hydraulic tables are more costly than standard models, the ease of control and the comfort it gives a groomer's neck and back more than make up for the initial investment. These efficient tables are useful for all dogs, particularly the large breeds.

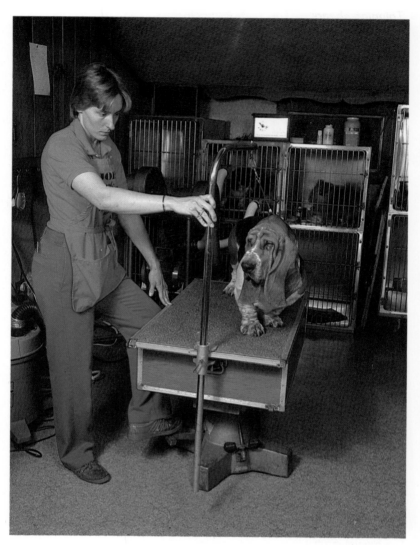

No professional should be without a hydraulic grooming table, complete with an adjustable grooming post and belly band loop.

- *Grooming posts* — Come in various styles and sizes. If you wish to do large dogs, the post should be at least 48″ high in order to give stability when raised to accommodate large dogs. Posts that go through the table (as opposed to those that fasten to the table edge) are most convenient, as you can move freely around the table without bumping into them or catching clipper cords on them. A second post can be attached to the back of the table in order to attach a "belly band" loop. This band prevents the dog

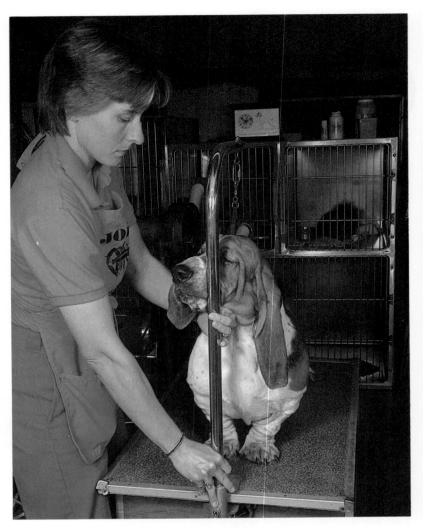

The grooming post is lowered to accommodate the Basset Hound, and the loop is placed around his neck—this keeps him still while he is being groomed.

from sitting down. Grooming loops should always be nylon and should have a secure lock—easy to open, but secure enough so that the dog cannot slip out easily.

- *Floor stand dryer* — Works well for blow drying on the table, as well as cage drying. A good-quality dryer should swivel and have a post that can be raised and lowered.
- *Cage dryer* — Attaches to the cage so that a dog may be dried in the cage.

Whether you use a floor stand dryer or a tabletop model, make certain to set the temperature to warm so as not to burn the dog's skin.

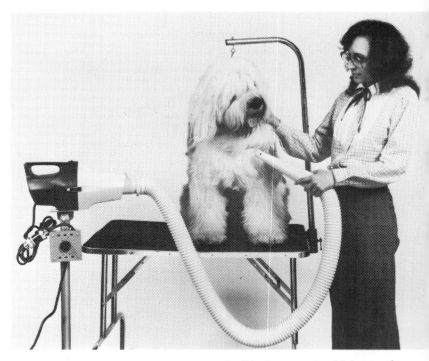

This groomer is using a dryer with a flexible hose and a high-speed wand nozzle to dry the shaggy Old English Sheepdog. The dryer can be unfastened from the stand and hand held.

- *High velocity dryer* — This dryer can be used while a dog is still in the tub. It blows the water down the hair shaft and off the hair with tremendous force. As it has no heating element, it uses very little electricity and cuts down tremendously on drying time.
- *Ramp* — A great aid for getting big dogs in the tub or on the table. Collapsible models fold up and can be stored when not in use.
- *Lather machine* — A machine that dispenses shampoo. Very economical to use, as it dispenses lather instead of liquid shampoo and it eliminates shampoo waste.
- *Oster A-2 clipper* — Blades on this clipper must be removed with a screw driver or you must have interchangeable heads. This clipper will accommodate the nail grinder.
- *Oster A-5* — Clipper with snap-on blades. Very serviceable, easy to maintain, and cuts through any coat.
- *Oster blades* — Made for both the A-2 and A-5 clipper. The higher the number, the closer it cuts. Blades are #30, #15, #10, #9, #8½, #7, #7F, #5, #5F, #4, #4F, #⅝, #⅞, and #⅜.
- *Oster spray lube* — Used to cool and lubricate blades and helps prevent blades from getting dull quickly.
- *Snap-on comb* — Comb-like attachment, available in various sizes,

40

which fits over the clipper head. As the coat is clipped, the hair will be uniformly cut to a predetermined, desired length.

- *Curved shears* — Used to achieve curved lines on a dog's coat, especially in the shoulder, flank, and chest areas.
- *Silk Handkerchief* — Used on short-haired white dogs to shine the coat.

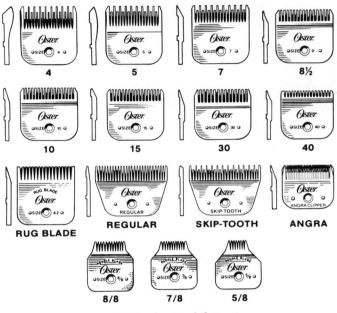

Blades for Model No. 2

There are clippers and blades for all grooming needs. The #10 blade, for example, clips hair to a medium length and works well on smooth coats, while the #5 blade is the best all-around blade for Poodles.

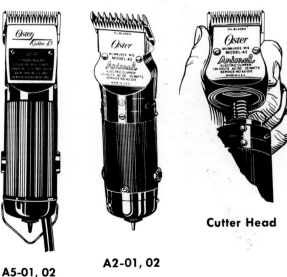

Cutter Head

A5-01, 02

A2-01, 02

2112-02

2112-31

Products such as a lubricant and blade wash (left) help to keep your clipping equipment clean and in good working order. Detachable cutting heads (bottom) allow you to change blades swiftly.

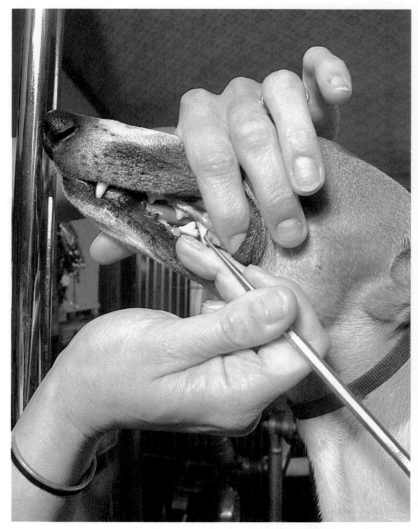

Tooth scaling, i.e., removing tartar and plaque from a dog's teeth, should be performed by a veterinarian, not a dog groomer.

Nylabone and Gumabone . . . Dogs Need to Chew

Part of the grooming job is examining and cleaning (in a very general way) a dog's teeth. Large accumulations can be removed simply with a scaler or probe, but this is NOT considered part of a grooming job and should be deferred for a veterinarian's technique. But you should examine the dog's teeth and report to the owner about their condition. Good teeth are clean and white, and you should not be able to scrape any residue off them.

Nylabone® products are the safest, most economical chew items you could ever give a dog. Not only do pet shops and veterinarians stock them, but so do most grooming salons.

Recommend and use Nylabone® or Gumabone® for dogs. These products have been around for 30 years or more. They have several unique advantages. First they can be used over and over again, being sterilized in between by boiling in chicken broth! This re-impregnates the flavor. Only use those products made by Nylabone Corp., as other bones melt if you boil them! By using Nylabone® as a pooch pacifier, the dogs do not agonize as much if they are left alone. For dogs whose teeth are too far gone to chew on Nyabone®, offer a Gumabone®. This is a softer (but very strong) material also made by the Nylabone Corporation. Many dogs prefer Gumabone® products, as they are chewier. Dogs are, by nature, destroyers. They chew from boredom and also to play. Once they have chewed a product apart they lose interest in it. Thus you should use excellent quality dog toys (like Nylabone® and Gumabone®) and stay away from vinyl squeeze toys, which dogs devastate in a few minutes.

Rawhide chews are also not to be recommended, as the dogs swallow them and they are basically indigestible. They are also unsanitary and are sources of filth and bacteria, because the dog's saliva softens and pre-digests them.

44

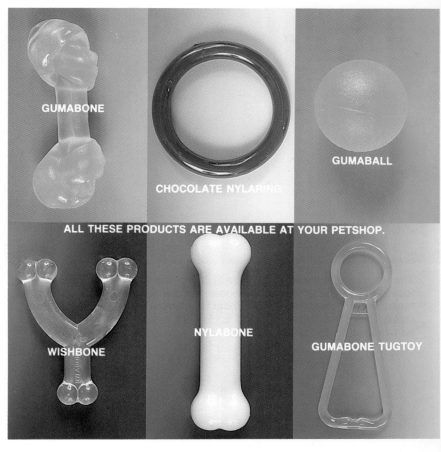

GUMABONE

CHOCOLATE NYLARING

GUMABALL

ALL THESE PRODUCTS ARE AVAILABLE AT YOUR PETSHOP.

WISHBONE

NYLABONE

GUMABONE TUGTOY

The Nylabone® Corporation manufactures chew products in every size and shape imaginable, including knots, rings, balls, wishbones, and tug-toys. There are several flavors available (chocolate and ham-scented are popular), depending on your dog's taste preferences! Unlike other chew toys—such as rawhide, vinyl, and rubber—Nylabone® and Guma-bone® products are more durable and won't break off into harmful chunks that a dog could swallow; they are more sanitary, as they can be boiled to remove harmful germs; and they are more economical, since they do not wear down as quickly as products made of other materials. Incidentally, if for some reason a dog *does* break off pieces of a Nylabone® chewing device (although this is highly unlikely), it means that you gave him too small a bone for his size. When in doubt, the bigger the bone the better.

The Maltese with the little red bows in its hair has been groomed to per-
fection in a style suitable for the show ring; the other two Maltese dogs
have been trimmed in a "Teddy bear" clip which renders a soft, fluffy,
cuddly look. The Teddy bear clip is ideal for pets, i.e., dogs that won't
be exhibited at dog shows.

THE TEDDY BEAR CLIP

Tools and Equipment
Slicker brush. Matting comb. Metal combs (medium/fine).
Medicated ear powder. Nail clipper. Oster A-5 clipper. #10, #15
blades. #1, #1½, #2 blade attachment combs (use
with a #30 blade). Cotton balls. Rubber bands. Scissors.

Grooming Procedure
- Using a #1, #1½, or #2 blade attachment comb (depending on
the length of the coat desired), clip the entire coat, starting at the
base of the skull from the base of the ears and from under the jaw
line (thus omitting the head, face, beard, and ears).
- 2. Fluff with the medium metal comb and scissor all ends evenly,
except the tail.

46

- 3. Comb forward the front ½" of hair on the head over the eyes and scissor evenly across the eyes. Scissor the head to blend into this line and continue to blend into the ears and the side of the face. (Note: The head, face, and beard should be scissored according to coat length on the body.)
- 4. Comb face and beard downward and scissor around from the base of each ear across the beard, thus forming a round "U" from the front.
- 5. Blend the sides of the face into the beard and around the "U" shape.
- 6. Comb through with the fine metal comb and scissor evenly all loose ends.
- 7. Finish the dog by scissoring the feet as before in the grooming instructions.

This type of clip can be used on Lhasa Apsos, Shih Tzus, Yorkshire Terriers, and certain mixed breeds where a cute, round, cuddly look is desired. After grooming, bathing, and fluff drying the dog, continue with the steps below. (Note: The #15 blade is for Yorkshire Terriers *only*, to shave the tips of the ears.)

THE MIXED BREED

Every dog has its day, or so the saying goes, and that surely has to be true about man's best friend, the "mutt" or mixed breed. Although mixed breeds are not purebred dogs, they have many of the desirable traits one looks for in a dog; as a result, they often make fine pets and household guardians.

Mixed breeds come in every shape and size with the larger Shepherd-mix types maintained and groomed as their namesakes or the Husky-type dogs groomed according to the thickness of their coat. Owners of the small to medium-sized mixed breeds (i.e., Terrier or Poodle-mix) realize it is just as important to have these dogs groomed on a regular basis as it for pure-bred. The Terrier-mixes tend to have hairy-textured coats, and these dogs can look good with a Wire Fox Terrier clip, for example. Many of the Poodle-mixes have wooly-textured coats and the owners of these dogs often prefer them in one of the Poodle clips (i.e., Lamb or Kennel clip). However, if a different style is desired for either the Terrier- or Poodle-mix, the groomer can appropriately clip the dog in what is known as a "Teddy Bear" clip.

Groomers should be encouraged to use their own discretion on the smaller mixed breed dogs—for example, Lhasapoos, Maltesepoos, Yorkiepoos, to name just a few. Generally, owners prefer a short, cuddly look that is easy to maintain.

When working on a dog, a groomer, sensing individuality, can decide on a round, cute face or a longer, more distinguished-looking face and adapt a "Teddy Bear" clip accordingly. A similar idea works for the Schnoodle (i.e., Schnauzer-Poodle) with some owners wanting a Schnauzer clip if the dog has a tendency to look more like this breed. If the dog has Schnauzer coloring, but has a wooly-textured coat, like that of a Poodle, again the groomer can always resort to the round, cuddly look of a teddy bear.

The thick-coated Cockapoos are hard to maintain in a Poodle Lamb clip—surely many groomers have had experience with this sort of coat, that of the American Cocker Spaniel/Poodle type. Cockapoos are generally more comfortable in a short style, and, depending on the owner's preferences, either a Kennel clip for a Poodle look or a suitable Teddy Bear clip (with the head and face scissored shorter) works well.

Another alternative for the mixed breeds is a Terrier head, either with eyebrows or a "visor" covering both eyes.

Affenpinscher

Tools and Equipment

Nail cutter (guillotine or scissor). Styptic powder. Ear cleaner. Cotton balls. Shampoo (all-purpose or texturizing). Slicker brush. Comb. Stripping knife. Straight shears. Blending shears.

Grooming Procedure

- Nails should be cut by removing only the tips; avoid cutting into the quick. If the nail should bleed, apply styptic powder to stop the bleeding. Any rough edges may be smoothed with a file.
- Using your fingers, pull out any hair that grows in the ear canal. Clean the ears with a liquid cleaner. Apply the cleaner to a cotton ball and wipe all accumulated dirt and wax out of the crevices of both ears.
- Brush out the entire dog with a slicker brush to remove dead coat and any mats.
- With the stripping knife pluck out the dead and loose hair that grows on the back until the hairs that are left are all a uniform length and lie flat. The hair on the neck, from the base of the skull down over the shoulders, to the elbows, across the rib cage, and down over the thighs should be plucked out as well.

- Bathe the dog in a shampoo of choice and rinse thoroughly.
- Towel dry the dog and finish drying him in a cage dryer.
- With straight shears cut the hair that grows in between the foot pads. Slightly round the paws.
- With blending shears remove the hair that grows on the outside of the ear leather from the base of the ear to the tip of the ear. With the straight shears cut the hair that sticks out past the edge of the ear even with the outer edge of the leather.
- With blending shears give the face a round appearance when viewed from the front. Excess hair growing from the corner of the eye may be removed as well.
- The legs may be shaped with the blending shears by removing any hair that is sticking out. This keeps them looking natural rather than scissored.
- The hair growing down from the chest should be shaped with blending shears, starting from the elbow and tapering slightly to the loin.
- Hair around the anus may be scissored. The tail may be neatened up with blending shears.

The Affenpinscher should appear neat without looking overly scissored. The natural look is in order for this breed, which should be groomed every 6 to 8 weeks.

Afghan Hound

Tools and Equipment
Large pin brush. Slicker brush. Steel comb. Matting comb. Matting rake. Nail cutter. Styptic powder. Ear cleaner. Cotton. Scissors. A-5 clipper/#10 blade. Coat dressing. Grooming spray.

Grooming Procedure
- The Afghan Hound is shown in its natural state. The coat is not clipped or trimmed. A thick, silky, fine-textured coat with close, short hair that forms a saddle along the back is the groomer's goal.
- Prior to bathing, the coat must be thoroughly brushed. This procedure removes all dead hair and eliminates all mats and tangles.
- Begin by lightly dampening a section of the coat with a good-quality coat dressing or mink oil conditioner. Brush with an upward motion using a large pin brush. Comb down with the teeth of the comb placed directly against the skin.
- Brushing out is the first and most important step in the grooming of an Afghan Hound. Thorough brushing before bathing requires the correct tools and a great deal of manual labor. The coat that is bathed when tangled or matted will be very difficult to work with. If a dog's coat is so badly matted that the dematting procedure would

be injurious to the animal, it is best to strip the coat and allow the new growth to be handled properly. The dog is less likely to become agitated if brushing begins at the hindquarters, doing rear leg and undersides, then the body sections, front legs next, and finally the head and tail.

- The nails are then cut. Doing so prior to bathing eliminates the possibility of too close a cut soiling—with blood or styptic powder—the cleaned foot.
- The ears should be swabbed out with a cotton pad moistened with a good-quality ear cleaner. At this time check for signs of infection.
- The bath follows, using the shampoo considered most appropriate for the animal's skin and coat condition.
- Fluff drying is the next step. When the coat is dry, again it should be checked with the comb for any snags or small tangles.
- The feet are now scissored around the outer edges to give a round appearance. The inner pad area is scissored to remove excess hair from the underside of the foot.
- The whiskers and long cheek hairs are removed with a #10 blade. Beards are left alone.
- The area of the coat above the hocks on the hind feet is parted and brushed forward. Coat dressing is applied to keep it in place.
- In the puppy styling, a part is formed from the eyes over the forehead and down to the tail. Once the saddle (a smooth strip of hair) grows in, only the head is parted. The neck and back hair lie naturally.

AIREDALE TERRIER

Tools and Equipment
Slicker brush. Metal comb (medium). Mat-splitting comb. Medicated ear powder. Large toenail clipper. Eye drops (eye stain remover). Cotton balls. Oster A-5 clipper. #10, «8½, #7, #5 blades. Scissors. Thinning shears.

Grooming Procedure
- Brush the entire coat and tail with the slicker brush. Comb through with the metal comb. (The coat texture varies from coarse and hairy to soft and cotton-like, the latter tending to mat.) Remove any mats with the mat-splitting comb.
- Clean the ears, using the medicated ear powder, and lightly pluck any stray hair from the insides.
- Moisten a cotton ball with eye drops and wipe the eyes clean. Some brands of eye drops also help remove any stains around the eyes.

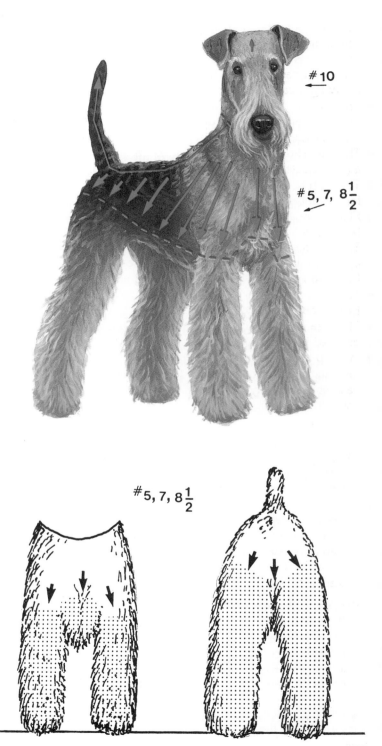

#10

#5, 7, 8½

#5, 7, 8½

- Cut the tips of the toenails with the large toenail clipper, being careful not to cut the quick.
- With the #10 blade on the Oster A-5 clipper, shave the head, starting at the center of the eyebrows, back to the base of the skull. (Note: When shaving the head, face, and throat, shave *with* the grain of the hair.) Then from the center again to the outer corner of the eyes. This line should be about ¾″ above the inner corner of the eye, tapering into the outer corner, thus making a triangle. Next shave down from the outer corners of the eyes to within ¾″ from the corners of the mouth and continue this line across, under the chin.
- Shave both sides of the ears, and from the back edge of the ears, shave down diagonally to a point at the base of the throat, thus forming a "V" shape.
- Shave the anal area, being certain not to put the blade in direct contact with the skin (⅛′¼″ each side).
- Shave abdomen area from groin to navel and down insides of thighs.
- With the #8½, #7, or #5 blade on the Oster A-5 clipper (according to the length of the coat desired) start at the base of the skull and clip down the back to the base of the tail.
- Clip the top half of the tail and blend down either side of the fringe. Comb the fringe downward and scissor the lower edge, thus making a feather shape.
- With the clipper, clip down the sides of the neck to the shoulder and down to the elbow.
- Clip down the chest to the breastbone and slope the pattern down diagonally to the center front of the legs.
- From the first clip down the back, clip down the sides of the stomach, arching the pattern over the hips. (From the side, the pattern line should slope down diagonally from the breastbone, straight across the tops of the front legs, sloping up across the stomach, arching up over the hips and down to a point in the rear.)
- Brush through the coat with the slicker brush to remove any excess hair.
- Place a cotton ball in each ear (this prevents any water from entering the ear canal) and bathe the dog. Cage dry him. (Note: For Airedales that have a cotton-like coat, it is recommended that you fluff dry the dog to prevent matting.)
- Brush and comb through the coat.
- Using the same blade on the Oster A-5 clipper as before, repeat the process for the pattern, blending the hair down from the top of the pattern, with the blade.
- Scissor around the edges of the ears.
- Scissor a "V" in the center of the eyebrows.

- Comb the hair on the face and eyebrows forward and downward. Align your scissors at an angle from the base of the nose to the outer corner of the eye. Scissor eyebrows from this angle, thus making a deep triangle (being careful not to cut any hair from the top of the muzzle).
- Lightly scissor stray hairs from around the edge and the sides of the beard. Using thinning shears, shape the beard, which should be long and barrel-shaped.
- Use thinning shears to trim any stray hairs from the top of the muzzle.
- Trim hair from between the foot pads, and while the dog is standing, scissor around the edges to give a round effect. (Note: Doing this first will give you a guide for scissoring the legs.)
- Scissor the front legs into straight tubular shapes.
- Scissor evenly the bottom of the chest fringe.
- Scissor the bottom of the belly fringe, following the contour of the dog's body, tapering up from the elbows on the front legs to the flanks at the rear.
- Scissor the rear legs, following the natural contours. (In rear view, the legs should be straight on the outside. On the inside, they should be straight, up to the thighs, and should arch up and into the shave line, thus forming the "Airedale Arch.")
- Lightly comb through the legs, fringes, and face, removing all excess hair and trimming any stray hairs as necessary.

The Airedale Terrier should be groomed every 6 to 8 weeks. The ears should be checked weekly and cleaned if necessary, and the toenails should be checked and cut at the grooming session.

AKITA

Tools and Equipment
Large pin brush. Metal rake (wide tooth). Metal comb (wide tooth). Medicated ear powder. Eye drops (eye stain remover). Slicker brush. Cotton balls. Scissors. Large nail clipper.

Grooming Procedure
- Starting at the head, brush the entire coat and tail with the slicker brush.
- With the metal rake, gently rake through the coat. During the non-shedding season, DO NOT rake out the undercoat; only untangle it with the rake, or metal comb.

- Clean the ears using medicated ear powder, and lightly pluck any stray hair from the insides.
- Clean the eyes by wiping with a cotton ball that has been moistened with eye drops. Certain eye drop products will also help in removing any stains.
- Clip the tip of each toenail with the nail clippers, being careful not to cut into the quick.
- With the scissors, clip the whiskers from the muzzle, the chin, the sides of the face, and above the eyes. (Note: Clipping the whiskers is a decision to be left to the owner.)
- Place a cotton ball in each ear (this prevents any water from entering the ear canal), and bathe the dog. Fluff dry him. You can also cage dry this dog first, drying most of the outer coat, and then fluff dry with the large pin brush.
- Brush through the coat briskly with the large pin brush, then comb through with the metal comb to remove the loosened hair.
- With the scissors, snip the hair from between the pads and toes on the feet and around the edges of each foot.

ALASKAN MALAMUTE

Tools and Equipment

Slicker brush. Steel comb (medium/fine). Pure boar bristle brush. Molting comb (#564) for shorthaired breeds. Scissors. Eye stain remover. Ear cleaner. Medicated ear powder. Protein coat conditioner. Tearless protein shampoo. Cotton balls. Nail clipper.

Grooming Procedure

• Spray the entire coat with protein coat conditioner. This adds body to the coat and helps repair split ends. Brush through the entire coat with the slicker brush to remove loose hair. Then, comb with the molting comb to take out loose undercoat.

• Swab the ears with a cotton ball moistened with ear cleaner. This will remove the dirt and control ear odor. Follow this with a dry cotton ball, and dust the ears with medicated ear powder.

• Cut the nails with a guillotine-type nail clipper. Nails should be cut monthly.

57

- Bathe the dog with a tearless protein shampoo that is pH-alkaline. This will add fullness and body to the coat and restructure damaged hair.
- Use a high velocity dryer to blow excess water off the dog while the dog is still in the tub. This will speed up the drying time and help prevent the coat from becoming overly dry. Cage dry the dog until the hair is damp. Then finish drying on the table, using a blow dryer and a pin brush to separate all of the hair and remove all of the loose coat. Finish with a steel comb through the entire coat, paying special attention to the fine hair behind the ears. Use the fine side of the comb for this area.
- Check between the foot pads and under the feet for burrs, tar, etc. Scissor the hair under the feet even with the pads. Trim around the paw and neaten the entire foot. Use thinning shears to trim the hair growing out from between the toes. Be sure to neaten the hair on the backs of the rear pasterns.
- The whiskers may be removed with scissors to improve expression (this is optional).
- Spray the entire coat with a protein coat conditioner to add brilliance and fragrance, and brush it in with the pure bristle brush.

AUSTRALIAN TERRIER

Tools and Equipment
Molting comb (for long hair). Pure boar bristle brush. Gentle slicker brush. Nail clipper (extra large). Ear cleaner. Medicated ear powder. Protein coat conditioner. Coat gloss. Fine face comb. Oster clipper. #10 blade. Stripping knife (medium/fine). Tearless protein shampoo. Cotton balls. Steel comb (medium/fine). Thinning shears, double edge. Scissors.

Grooming Procedure
- Spray the dog with coat gloss to lubricate the coat and prevent hair loss. Brush with a gentle slicker brush and then comb thoroughly with a molting comb to remove dead undercoat.
- Swab the ears with a cotton ball moistened with ear cleaner. This will remove the dirt and control ear odor. Follow this with a dry cotton ball and dust the ears with medicated ear powder.
- Cut the nails with a guillotine-type nail trimmer. Nails should be cut monthly.

- Check between the foot pads and under the feet for burrs, tar, and so forth. Scissor the hair under the feet to prevent debris from adhering. Trim any hair around the paw that touches the ground or grows out between the paws with thinning shears.
- Trim the hair around the anus with a scissor and remove any long hair under the tail that hangs over the anus and may become soiled.
- Bathe the Aussie with a tearless terrier shampoo that adds body and texture to the hair and does not soften the coat.
- Cage dry until the hair is damp and finish drying on the table using a blow dryer and a stiff, natural bristle brush. Spray with coat gloss to eliminate flyaway hair and static. Brush the coat straight from neck to tail, with no part. Then brush down over the shoulders and sides. Comb thoroughly with the medium side of the steel comb.
- Clip the stomach area with a #10 blade, going *with* the grain.
- Dead, straggly hair should be removed from the neck, body, and tail with a medium stripping knife or with the thumb and fingers.
- Tidy the dog's hind parts and rear legs. Blend the coat slightly from stifle to hocks. Trim close from hock to foot with thinning shears.
- The hair on the underside of the tail should be trimmed short. Remove dead, straggly hair from the tail tip and blend the tail into the back. If the tail is short, leave hair beyond the tip to lengthen; if long, trim close to the tip.
- From the tail on each side and on the back of the hip, blend the coat down to the cowlick on the back of each leg.

59

- Never flatten the topknot. Train up with a brush and a fine-toothed comb (use face comb).
- Strip long, surplus hair on the face and cheeks. Pluck with the fingers around the ears, between the eyes, and slightly under the eyes to enhance expression. This can be done with thinning shears also.
- Clean the black, leathery space on the bridge of the muzzle in a V-shape.
- Whiskers can be removed.
- Strip or pluck the back of the ears so that they are free of long hair—usually one-third to two-thirds down to the base—and trim very close. Outside edges are to be trimmed neat and sharp. Ears can be clipped with a #10 blade.
- Use a medium stripping knife to lightly strip the back of the neck, to emphasize length, blending into the shoulders and body.
- Strip slightly underneath the chin to about the center of the underjaw. Comb the muzzle forward.
- Brush the ruff out from under the throat to the shoulders to create a bib-like ruff. Chest should be combed down to form an apron.
- Trim excessive long hair from the front legs with thinning shears. Leave feathering on the back of the legs. Excessive tufts around the elbows should be removed. Trim close from the hock joint down.
- Trim the feet with scissors to neaten.
- If showing, bathe the Aussie at least four days before the show.
- Spray your pure bristle brush with protein coat conditioner and top brush the coat to add brilliance and fragrance.

BASSET HOUND

Tools and Equipment

Short bristle brush (or very gentle slicker). Shedding blade. Hound glove. Nail cutter. Styptic powder. Ear cleaner. Cotton. Mineral oil. Baby powder. Lanolin coat conditioner. Scissors.

Grooming Procedure

- The Basset Hound is shown in a coat that is short and smooth. The skin should be loose and elastic.
- Prior to bathing the coat should be brushed thoroughly to remove all dead hair. If heavy shedding is evident, a shedding blade may be stroked lightly over the coat or a curry brush may be used in a circular motion prior to brushing.

- Next the inner ear is cleaned by swabbing with a cotton pad that has been moistened with a good-quality ear cleaner. Check the ears for signs of infection. The Basset's long ears might have crusted · edges due to dried-on food debris. These edges can be moistened with mineral oil before bathing. The flews and deep haws also should be checked for blistering or food debris.
- The nails are then clipped.
- The bath, with proper shampoo for skin type and coat conditioner, is the next step. Any discolored white areas of the coat will benefit from an application of a bluing rinse (one cup laundry bluing to three quarts water) before the final rinsing is done.
- The Basset Hound can be cage dried.
- After drying, the hair on the underside of the foot pads is scissored.
- All facial whiskers are scissored. The facial wrinkles should be checked to make certain they are thoroughly dry. An application of baby powder in these areas will keep them from becoming irritated.
- The tail feathering is not removed.
- Application of a lanolin coat conditioner is the final step. Put a few drops of the conditioner in your hands, rub your hands together, and gently massage this into the coat.

BEAGLE

Tools and Equipment
Short bristle brush. Curry brush. Ear cleaner. Cotton. Nail cutter. Styptic powder. Scissors. Thinning shears. Lanolin coat conditioner.

Grooming Procedure
- The Beagle is shown in a coat that is close, hard, and glossy. Prior to bathing, the coat should be brushed thoroughly to remove all dead hair. A curry brush used in a circular motion may precede brushing.
- Next the inner ear is cleaned by swabbing with a cotton pad that has been moistened with a good-quality ear cleaner. Check for signs of ear infection.
- The nails are clipped.
- The bath, with proper shampoo for skin type and coat conditioner, is the next step. Any discolored white areas of the coat will benefit from an application of a bluing rinse (one cup laundry bluing to three quarts water) before the final rinsing is done.
- The Beagle can be cage dried.
- The facial whiskers may be scissored. Thinning shears might be necessary on the neck from the bottom of the ear corner to the front of the shoulder.
- Application of a lanolin coat conditioner is the final step.

62

BEARDED COLLIE

Tools and Equipment
Large pin brush. Slicker brush. Steel comb (medium/fine). Long-hair molting comb (#565). Wood utility comb (matting comb). Pure boar bristle brush. Scissors. Nail clipper (extra large). High velocity dryer. Ear forceps. Coat gloss. Protein coat conditioner. Tearless protein shampoo. Tearless whitening shampoo. Ear cleaner. Cotton balls. Eye stain remover. Medicated ear powder.

Grooming Procedure
- Spray the entire coat with protein coat conditioner. This adds body to the coat and helps repair split ends. If the coat is matted in areas, spray the matted areas with tangle remover. Let the dog sit 10 to 15 minutes with both products on the coat until they are absorbed and the coat is partially dry.
- After 15 minutes, spray the entire coat with coat gloss. This lubricates the coat for easier brushing and combing and prevents hair breakage. Brush through the entire coat with the pin brush, using a slicker brush and the utility comb in the matted areas of the coat. Start at the rear of the dog at the bottom of the skirt area. Work in sections, lifting the hair and brushing it layer by layer. Mist

each section with coat gloss as you work. Never brush a dry-coated Bearded Collie. Work through the entire coat from the back to the neck area.

- To get a nice natural part along the spine, comb all of the undercoat out along the spine. The top coat will then lie flat, naturally parted. The coat should fall naturally to either side. Comb hair down on each side. Never bathe this breed with mats in the coat, as water tends to tighten mats and make them harder to remove.
- Swab the ears with a cotton ball that has been moistened with ear cleaner. This will remove the dirt and control ear odor. Follow this with a dry cotton ball and dust the ears with medicated ear powder. Pull out any dead hair inside the ears with your fingers or ear forceps.
- Cut the nails with a guillotine-type nail trimmer. Nails should be cut monthly.
- Check between the foot pads and under the feet for burrs, tar, etc. Scissor the hair under the foot even with the pads to prevent debris from adhering. Trim any hair around the paw that the dog walks on.
- Scissor any long hair under the tail that hangs over the anus and that may become soiled with feces. Scissor the hair around the anus and be sure the opening is clear. Trim or blend down the area under the tail if it is profuse; otherwise, it may collect feces and become a nidus for infection.
- Bathe the dog with a tearless protein shampoo that is pH-alkaline. This will add fullness and body to the coat and restructure damaged hair. Use the whitener shampoo on white areas of the coat.
- Use a high velocity dryer to blow excess water off the dog while the dog is still in the tub. This will speed up the drying time and help prevent the coat from becoming overly dry.
- Allow the dog to sit and air dry for about 30 minutes, but do not use the dryer as it may dry areas and cause curling. Next dry the dog on the table, using a blow dryer set to "warm" and using a pin brush to separate and straighten the entire coat for a smooth, silky look.
- Be sure to brush down to the skin and follow this by combing with a long-tooth steel comb.
- Scissor around the outside edges of the feet to make them oval and neat. Hair is left between the toes, and the feet are to be well covered with hair. Depending on the dog's environment and living conditions, profuse hair between the foot pads and toes can be scissored for cleanliness.
- The skull should be broad and flat, so straggly hair can be removed to conform with the desired appearance.

- Pluck hair from the inside corner of the eyes and the stop. Pluck the hair out over the eyes until a nice arch is shaped to add to the inquiring expression this breed is to have. Hair over the eyes is combed up and to the sides to frame the eyes and blend smoothly into the coat on the sides of the head.
- The bridge of the nose is sparsely covered with hair, which should be combed down on each side of the muzzle to form the typical beard.
- Ears are to be long and natural.
- The neck should blend smoothly into the shoulders. Clumps of hair in this area may be thinned with thinning shears. Always use thinning shears in combination with a comb. Hold thinning shears pointed in the direction the hair grows. Thin out and comb the hair to achieve the desired look. Never cut across the grain.
- Brush each side of the body hair *down* to encourage the natural part.
- The topline should be straight and the tail set low. If the dog's rear is higher than his front and you have profuse hair on the rear, you can lower the back end by thinning the rump with thinning shears.
- Brush the chest down and the hair on the legs straight down.
- Brush the tail into a full plume.
- Spray a protein coat conditioner (with mink oil) lightly from above and allow it to mist over the coat. Brush with a pure bristle brush. The spraying and brushing gives the coat a beautiful gloss and aroma.

It should be noted that a coat which has been trimmed *in any way* must be seriously penalized and a sculptured coat is a serious fault. The grooming instructions listed above are to make a Bearded Collie a more enjoyable member of the family; they are not intended for show dogs.

BEDLINGTON TERRIER

Tools and Equipment
Slicker brush. Mat-splitting comb. Metal comb (medium). #15, #10, #4, #5 blades. Eye drops (eye stain remover). Cotton balls. Oster A-5 clipper. Medicated ear powder. Scissors. Toenail clipper.

Grooming Procedure
- Brush the entire coat with the slicker brush, removing any mats with the mat-splitting comb.

- Clean the ears using the medicated ear powder and lightly pluck any stray hair from the insides.
- Clean the eyes by wiping with a cotton ball that has been moistened with eye drops. If the eyes are excessively sticky and watering, with scissors, snip the stained hair from the corners of the eyes.
- Cut the tips of the toenails with the toenail clipper, being careful not to cut the quick.
- With the #15 blade on the Oster A-5 clipper, shave the face, starting at the front edge of the ears straight to the outer corners of the eyes. From the outer corners of the eyes shave straight down to within ½" from the corners of the mouth. Next shave from the back edges (base) of the ears, diagonally down to a point at the base of the throat, thus forming a "V" shape. (Note: When shaving the face, chin, and throat, shave *against* the grain of the hair.)
- Shave the entire underjaw.
- Shave the ears from the base to within 1" from the center of the edge and down both sides of the ear diagonally from the first point, making an inverted "V" shape.
- With the #10 blade shave the anal area, being certain not to put the blade in direct contact with the skin (½" on each side).
- Shave the stomach area from the groin to the naval and down the insides of the thighs.
- With the #15 blade shave ⅔ of the tail from the tip, leaving ⅓ of the hair at the base. Shave the underside of the remaining ⅓ of the tail.
- With the #4 or #5 blade on the clipper (according to the length of coat desired) start at the base of the ears and clip diagonally toward the center of the base of the neck, thus making a "V" from the base of the ears down into the neck. Then clip down the back to the base of the tail.
- Clip down the sides of the neck to the shoulders and blend the hair down into the top of the front legs.
- Clip down the chest to the breastbone.
- From the first clip down the back, clip down the sides of the stomach.
- Blend the hair from the top of the back on the rear end into the top of the thighs.
- Brush through the hair on the legs, head, and face to remove any excess hair.
- Putting a cotton ball in each ear prevents any water from entering the ear canal. Bathe the dog and towel dry.
- Place the dog on the grooming table and fluff dry with the slicker brush, brushing the hair in an upward motion to make it full.
- Using the same blade on the Oster A-5 clipper as before, repeat the process on the face and body.

Scissor the shaved edges of the ears, comb the "tassels" down, and scissor the lower edges into a curve.

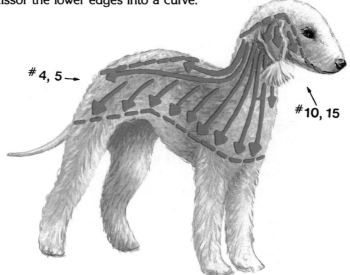

#4, 5 →

#10, 15

- Scissor the head into the "Roman Arch," i.e., arching from the nose up and over the head and ending in a "V" on the neck. Scissor the sides to curve down and taper into the bases of the ears.
- Scissor the muzzle around so that it is in proportion with the head. When viewed from the front, the head should appear long and straight, arching across the top between the ears, and tapering slightly on the muzzle.
- Scissor the remaining ⅓ on the top of the tail into a tubular shape, blending into the body.
- Scissor around the shave lines on the throat and stomach.
- Trim the hair from between the pads of the feet; and while the dog is standing, scissor around the edges of the feet to give a round effect. (Doing this first will give you a guide for scissoring the legs.)
- Scissor the chest, between the legs and underneath the stomach.
- Scissor the front legs into straight, tubular shapes.
- Scissor the rear legs, following the natural contours. The insides should be straight to the hock joint and taper on up to the shave line.
- Lightly comb through and fluff up the hair on the legs, head, muzzle, and tail, making sure they are even. Trim any stray hairs as necessary.

The Bedlington Terrier should be groomed every 6 or 8 weeks. Regular brushing and combing by the owner between groomings will help prevent mats. The ears should be checked weekly and cleaned if necessary, and the toenails should be checked and cut at the grooming session.

67

BORDER TERRIER

Tools and Equipment
Slicker brush. Pure boar bristle brush. Steel comb
(medium/coarse). Stripping knife. Thinning scissors. Ear forceps.
Nail clipper. Ear cleaner. Medicated ear powder. Cotton balls.
Tearless terrier shampoo. Protein coat conditioner.

Grooming Procedure
- Brush the coat with a pure boar bristle brush to stimulate the
  growth of new coat and to thin down the undercoat. Use the slicker
  brush on heavy areas and to help remove dead undercoat. Comb
  thoroughly with the coarse side of the comb.
- Swab the ears with a cotton ball moistened with ear cleaner. This
  will remove dirt and control ear odor. Follow with a dry cotton ball
  and dust the ears with medicated ear powder. To remove stray hair
  inside the ears, pluck with your fingers or use ear forceps.
- Cut the nails with a guillotine-type nail trimmer. Nails should be cut
  monthly.
- Check between the foot pads and under the feet for burrs, tar, etc.
  Scissor the hair under the foot even with the pads to prevent debris
  from adhering. With a thinning shear, trim any hair around the paw
  that touches the ground or grows out between the toes. Do not
  expose the nails.

- Trim the hair around the anus with a scissor and remove any long hair under the tail that hangs over the anus and that may become soiled.
- Bathe the dog with a tearless terrier shampoo that adds body and texture to the hair and does not soften the coat.
- Cage dry until damp. Finish drying on the table using a blow dryer and a pure bristle brush. Thoroughly comb the entire dog with a medium comb.
- Use a stripping knife or thinning shears to remove the hair between the ears and the excess hair on the side of the head and cheeks. The skull should be clean and look broad between the ears, and the hair should blend from the head into the throat without looking clumpy. If you use the stripping knife, use it only for the purpose of gripping the hair and not cutting it. The hair is pulled in the direction of the natural lie of the hair, never against the grain.
- The ears should look clean and smooth. Remove wisps of hair at the top of the ears, fringes on the ears, and long hair on the edges by pulling with your fingers. Do not cut with scissors. The hair pulls out quite easily.
- The eyebrow pencil line at the outer corner of the eye should show. Use a scissor to trim the eyebrow short. No hair should protrude away from the eye at the outside corner. The eye should have clear vision, so pluck out any hair on the stop that protrudes in front of the eye. Do not strip out in front of the cheeks.
- Trim straggly hair in the moustache and whiskers.
- With thinning shears, tip any straggly hair on the neck and back, under the neck, on the brisket, between the front legs, and on the belly. Neaten and define the tuck-up. Point the shears down and angle under the dog toward the feet on the opposite side. Tipping helps the coat stand up and out.
- Trim inside the thigh on the rear legs and from the crotch down. Tip the rear hock to create a perpendicular line from hock to ground. Comb and remove stray hairs that are down the front portion of the leg, rounding the leg and defining the stifle. The lower portion of the rear leg should form a cylinder when viewed from any angle.
- Tip straggly hair on the front legs and shape the feet to give a rounded appearance. Blend the feet into the leg furnishings.
- Thin the tail at the base to make it blend smoothly into the body. Remove any long fringes on the underside of the tail with thinning shears. Taper the tail to a rounded point at the end.
- Top brush the coat with a pure bristle brush sprayed with protein coat conditioner to add brilliance and fragrance.

BORZOI

Tools and Equipment

Nail cutter (guillotine or scissor). Styptic powder. Ear cleaner. Cotton balls. Shampoo (conditioning or whitening). Slicker brush. Comb. Straight scissor. Spray conditioner or coat gloss.

Grooming Procedure

- Nails should be cut by removing only the tips and avoiding the quick. If the nail should bleed, apply styptic powder to stop the bleeding. Any rough nail edges may be smoothed with a nail file.
- Clean the ears with a liquid cleaner. Apply the cleaner to a cotton ball and wipe all accumulated dirt and wax from all crevices in both ears.
- Brush through the entire dog to remove any matted or dead hair.
- Bathe the dog in the shampoo of your choice. Rinse thoroughly. A creme rinse may be used to help cut down on static electricity.
- Towel dry the dog. A high velocity dryer may be used at this time to blow off excess water from the coat. Finish drying with a regular blow dryer while brushing the coat in the direction of its growth. When the hair on the very top of the back is just damp dry, complete the drying while brushing the coat *against* the growth to make the hair stand more erect. This helps to accentuate the distinctive topline. When the dog is dry, comb through the coat to check for any tangles that might have been missed.
- With scissors remove hair from between the foot pads and any excess hair on the bottom of the foot. The hair on the pasterns and the hocks may be neatened up also.
- The whiskers, along with the eyebrows, may be removed if desired, and any tufts of hair sticking out from the ears may also be removed.

BOSTON TERRIER

Tools and Equipment

Pure boar bristle brush. Ear cleaner. Medicated ear powder. Nail clipper. Scissors. Eye stain cleaner. Baby Powder or talcum powder. Mink oil. Tearless protein shampoo. Coarse hand towel. Cotton balls. Fine thinning shear.

Grooming Procedure

- Brush with a pure boar bristle brush.
- Swab ears with a cotton ball that has been moistened with ear cleaner. This will remove dirt and control ear odor. Follow with a dry cotton ball and dust the ears with medicated ear powder.
- Cut the nails with a guillotine-type nail clipper. Nails should be cut monthly.
- Check between the foot pads and under the feet for burrs, tar, etc.
- Wipe inside the corners of the eyes with a water-moistened cotton ball. Remove any eye stains under and around the eyes with a cotton ball that has been moistened with eye stain cleaner.
- Wrinkles on the face should be cleaned with a water-moistened cotton ball. Dry and powder.
- Bathe with a tearless protein shampoo that is pH-alkaline. This will add body to the coat and restructure damaged hair.

71

- Cage dry till damp. Finish drying on the table using a blow dryer and a pure bristle brush.
- The whiskers may be removed with a scissor to improve expression (optional).
- Any hair that detracts from the sleek appearance, or any dark hair that overlaps white areas of the coat, can be scissored. Use a fine thinning shear. To improve appearance, smooth out any overly-heavy patches of hair.
- Finish with a mist of mink oil to create a brilliant shine. To maintain the dark coat, use mink oil with PABA sunscreen to reduce fading. Just polish with a coarse towel.

BOUVIER DES FLANDRES

Tools and Equipment

Slicker brush. Large pin brush. Pure boar bristle brush. Steel comb (medium/coarse). Long hair molting comb (#565). Scissors. Cotton balls. Stripping knife. Thinning shear. Ear cleaner. Medicated ear powder. Mink oil. High velocity dryer. Nail clipper (extra-large). Tearless protein shampoo. Oster A-5 clipper. #10 blade.

Grooming Procedure

- Spray the entire coat with protein coat conditioner. This adds body to the coat and helps repair split ends. Brush through the entire coat with a slicker brush. Start at the rear of the dog, at the bottom of the skirt area. Work in sections through entire dog from the back to the neck area. Comb the entire coat with the molting comb to pull out dead undercoat. Starting at the head, back brush the entire coat with the pin brush. Then brush it back into place. Brush the legs up and then down.
- Swab the ears with a cotton ball that has been moistened with ear cleaner. This will remove the dirt and control ear odor. Follow this with a dry cotton ball, and dust the ears with medicated ear powder.
- Cut the nails with a guillotine-type nail clipper. Nails should be cut monthly.
- Check between the foot pads and under the feet for burrs, tar, etc. Clip the hair between the pads of the feet with a #10 blade. Trim any hair around the paws that touch the ground, and neaten the entire foot.
- Bathe the dog with a tearless terrier shampoo. This will add texture and body to the coat, yet it won't soften the coat.
- Use a high velocity dryer to blow excess water off the dog while he is still in the tub. This will speed up the drying time and help prevent the coat from becoming overly dry. Cage dry the dog until the hair is damp. Then, finish drying on the table using a blow dryer and a pin brush to separate all the hair and remove all of the loose coat. Finish by combing through the entire coat with a steel comb.
- Shave the ears on both sides with a #10 blade. Shave from base to tip. Trim the outside edge, using the thumb as a protective guide to prevent nicks. Give a neat appearance, forming a sharply defined line on the outer edge of the ears. Ears should stand out from the ruff of the neck.
- Shorten the hair on the crown of the head and at the sides of the face so that there is good contrast between the head and ears. Do it with a coarse stripping knife, taking the hair firmly between the thumb and edge of the knife. Turn the blade and pull a few hairs at a time in the direction of hair growth. You may also pluck the hair. Pluck by holding hair between the thumb and index finger, turning your wrist and pulling at the same time. Stripping or plucking keeps the coat uneven and natural looking. *Do not use clippers or scissors to shorten this area.* Skull hair should be removed just above the eyebrows, back across the skull and blending into the longer hair behind the ears.
- Cheeks should be flattened from the back corner of the eye and the corner of the mouth. Comb and strip, if necessary, the side of the cheeks to avoid protruding cheeks.

- Eyebrows are long and erect. Comb forward over the eyes. Accentuate by slightly parting with stripping knife. Eyes should be visible. Shape the eyebrows to give expression. Scissor diagonally from the outside corner to the center of the eye. *Do not trim or remove hair between the eyes;* comb it down over the muzzle.
- Brush the Bouvier's beard outward and upward to give width to the muzzle. At the bottom of the beard, divide the hair in half from the middle of the jaw and comb outward and forward to add width. Neaten the beard but leave it very thick.
- Comb the throat and chest hair down. Use a thinning shear to taper the hair toward the shoulder on either side. This gets the coat to lie smoothly and blend into the shoulders.
- Comb in the direction the hair grows. Comb the back and upper side to the rear. Comb the lower side down.
- The brisket is deep, at least to the point of the elbow, with nice tuck-up. Use thinning shears to form and neaten the tuck-up. Point shears down and angled under the leg toward the feet on the opposite side.
- With scissors remove hair that covers the anus and trim hair on the underside of the tail. Shorten the coat at the back of the rump with a thinning shear.
- Scissor around the circumference of the foot to develop a cat's paw.
- Comb the front legs straight down. Strip out tufts of excess hair at the elbows. Neaten the legs to give a massive, clean line.
- Comb the rear legs straight down. Thin excess hair at the breeches. Comb hocks back and remove wild hair with a scissor.
- This breed should look neat and clean but never over-trimmed.
- Finish with a mist of mink oil to create a brilliant shine, and brush it in with a pure boar bristle brush.

Owners requesting a shorter coat and less coat to maintain may ask that this breed be clipped. If so, use an 8½" blade, on the head and blend the body down with a #4 blade; or for a longer, nicer look, use a #10 blade and a one guard. Clipped areas are blended into patterned areas above to achieve a similar look.

BOXER

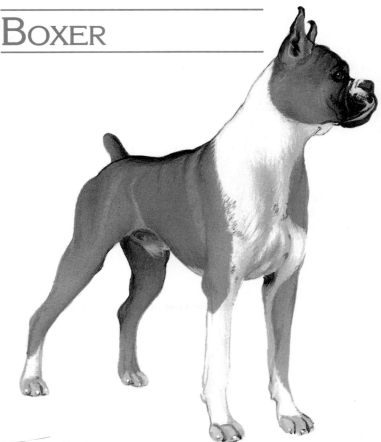

Tools and Equipment

Nail cutter (scissor or guillotine). Styptic powder. Ear cleaner.
Cotton balls. Shampoo (all-purpose or conditioning). Rubber brush.
Hard rubber curry brush. Blending shears. Straight shears. Spray
conditioner.

Grooming Procedure

- Nails should be cut by removing the tips; avoid cutting the quick. If
  the nail bleeds, apply styptic powder to stop the bleeding. Any
  rough nail edges may be smoothed by filing.
- Clean the ears with a liquid cleaner. Apply cleaner to a cotton ball
  and wipe accumulated wax and dirt from all crevices in both ears.
- Bathe the dog in your shampoo of choice. A whitening shampoo
  may be used on any white areas. To help remove dead hair while
  bathing, use the rubber brush to lather the dog. Rinse the dog
  thoroughly. An after-bath conditioner rinse may be applied to help
  control dandruff.
- Towel dry the dog and place him in a cage with a dryer until he is
  completely dry.

- When the dog is dry, any additional dead hair may be removed with the curry brush. Rub the dog with the curry in circular motions against the lay of hair.
- With small straight shears remove hair from the edges of the ears. Whiskers and eyebrows may be removed at an owner's request; otherwise they may be left alone. Hair in the tuck-up area and under the tail may be trimmed with straight shears. Any seams (where two different directions of hair growth come together) may be blended with blending shears.
- As the final step, spray a small amount of spray conditioner or coat gloss on the dog and buff to a shiny gloss with a clean cloth.

The properly groomed Boxer should have a crisp outline with a shiny coat, which lies smooth and tight to the body. This grooming should be done every 10 to 12 weeks.

BRITTANY SPANIEL

Tools and Equipment
Slicker brush. Steel comb (fine/medium). Pure boar bristle brush. Hound glove. Short hair molting comb (#564). Scissor. Pin brush. Thinning shear. Oster A-5 clipper. Stripping knife. Ear cleaner. Medicated ear powder. Protein coat conditioner. High velocity dryer. Tearless protein shampoo. Cotton balls. Nail clipper. #10 blade. #7 blade.

Grooming Procedure
- Spray the entire coat with protein coat conditioner. This adds body to the coat and helps repair split ends. Brush through the entire coat with the molting comb. This will remove the dead undercoat. Start at the rear of the dog at the bottom of the skirt area. Work through the entire dog from the back to the neck area. Then brush through the coat with a slicker brush to remove the top dead coat. Work vigorously. The more hair you remove now, the less hair you need to wash and dry.
- Swab the ears with a cotton ball that has been moistened with ear cleaner. This will remove the dirt and control ear odor. Follow this with a dry cotton ball and dust the ears with medicated ear powder.

- Cut the nails with a guillotine-type nail clipper. Nails should be cut monthly.
- Check between the foot pads and under the feet for burrs, tar, etc. Scissor the hair under the feet to prevent debris from adhering. With a thinning shear, trim any hair around the paw that touches the ground or grows out between the paws.
- Use a #10 blade to clip the hair around the anus. Just clear the area and do not use heavy pressure. Scissor any long hair under the tail that hangs over the anus and that may become soiled.
- Bathe the dog with a tearless protein shampoo that is pH-alkaline. This will add fullness and body to the coat and restructure damaged hair.

- Use a high velocity dryer to blow excess water off the dog while the dog is still in the tub. This will speed up the drying time and help prevent the coat from becoming overly dry. Cage dry the dog until the hair is damp. Then, finish drying on the table, using a blow dryer and a pin brush to separate all the hair and remove all of the loose coat.
- To keep the coat flat and give a more sleek appearance, pin a large towel around the dog while it is drying. Leave the towel on until the dog is almost completely dry.
- Brush the entire coat with a pin brush and be sure to brush to the skin, using the dryer to style and separate the hair. Follow by

combing the entire coat in the natural direction of the hair growth to encourage a flat, sleek look. Use the fine part of the comb on the soft hair behind the ears.

- The whiskers may be removed with scissors to improve the expression (optional).
- Use a stripping knife to remove any straggly hair on the top of the head, around the ears, and under the neck. With thinning shears, blend the hair where the ear joins the skull. Use a thinning shear on the underside of the ear to encourage the ear to lie close to the head.
- Blend the neck and shoulders to lie smooth. Use the thinning shear to blend lower the hair under the neck to the breastbone. There should be no thick ruff left, just a smooth taper.
- Lightly strip any straggly hair on the back. This can also be carded out, holding a #15 blade in your hand and stripping through the coat. Any work on the back should not be noticeable. You should remove only hair that does not conform to the overall desired outline.
- Use the thinning shear if the leg feathering is profuse; scissor the feathering evenly, creating a taper. Remove any long, uneven hair from the hock down to the bottom of the foot.
- Spray your pure bristle brush with protein coat conditioner and top brush the coat to add brilliance and fragrance.

BULLDOG

Tools and Equipment
Nail cutter (guillotine or scissor). Styptic powder. Ear cleaner. Cotton balls. Shampoo (all-purpose or whitening). Rubber brush. Hound glove. Scissors. Spray conditioner or coat gloss.

Grooming Procedure
- Nails should be cut by removing the tips only; avoid cutting the quick. If the nail should bleed, apply styptic powder to stop the bleeding. Any rough nail edges may be smoothed with a file.
- Clean the ears with a liquid ear cleaner. Apply the cleaner to a cotton ball and remove all accumulated dirt and wax from the

crevices of both ears.
- Bathe the dog in your shampoo of choice. Special attention should be given to the folds of the skin around the face, legs, and body. The rubber brush may be used to lather the dog and to help remove dead hair. Rinse the dog thoroughly.
- Towel dry the dog and continue drying him with a blow dryer. The dog may be cage dried.
- Brush the dog with a hound brush to remove dead hair and to make the coat lie smooth.
- Apply a light spray of coat conditioner or coat gloss and buff with a clean cloth until shiny.
- Whiskers may be removed with scissors if desired.

The Bulldog should be groomed every 8 to 12 weeks.

CARDIGAN WELSH CORGI

Tools and Equipment

Slicker brush (gentle). Steel comb (medium/fine). Pure boar bristle brush. Short hair molting comb (#564). Scissor. Eye stain remover. Ear cleaner. Medicated ear powder. Protein coat conditioner. Tearless protein shampoo. Cotton balls. Nail clipper.

Grooming Procedure
- Spray the entire coat with protein coat conditioner. This adds body to the coat and helps repair split ends. Brush through the entire coat with the gentle slicker to remove loose hair. Then, to take out loose undercoat, comb with the molting comb made for short-haired breeds (#564).
- Swab the ears with a cotton ball that has been moistened with ear cleaner. This will remove dirt and control ear odor. Follow this with a dry cotton ball and dust the ears with medicated ear powder.
- Cut the nails with a guillotine-type nail clipper. Nails should be cut monthly.
- Bathe the dog with a tearless protein shampoo that is pH-alkaline. This will add fullness and body to the coat and restructure damaged hair.
- Cage dry until damp. Finish drying on the table using a blow dryer and a pure bristle brush. Comb the entire dog thoroughly.
- Check between the foot pads and under the feet for burrs, tar, etc. Scissor the hair under the feet even with the pads. Trim any hair around the paw that touches the ground and neaten the entire foot. Use thinning shears to trim the hair growing out from between the toes. Be sure to neaten the hair on the back of the rear pasterns.
- Scissor any long hair under the tail that hangs over the anus. Be sure the anus is clear and then trim down under the tail area so it does not become soiled.
- The whiskers may be removed with scissors to improve the expression (optional).
- Top brush with a pure bristle brush sprayed with protein coat conditioner to add brilliance and fragrance.

CHESAPEAKE BAY RETRIEVER

Tools and Equipment
Nail cutter (guillotine or scissor). Styptic powder. Ear cleaner. Cotton balls. Shampoo (all-purpose). Slicker brush.

Grooming Procedure
- Cut the nails by removing only the tips. Avoid cutting the quick. If the nail should bleed, apply styptic powder until the bleeding stops.
- Clean the ears with a liquid ear cleaner by applying the cleaner to a cotton ball and wiping all accumulated wax and dirt from the crevices of both ears.
- Brush out the entire dog with a slicker brush to remove any loose or dead hair.
- Bathe the dog in your shampoo of choice. Lather well and rinse the dog thoroughly.
- Towel off excess water and finish drying in a cage dryer.

This breed needs no additional grooming, although the whiskers and eyebrows may be removed if desired. A brush may be run through the coat to make it lie close. The Chessie should be groomed every 8 to 12 weeks.

CHIHUAHUA, LONG COAT

Tools and Equipment
Nail cutter (scissor or guillotine). Styptic powder. Ear cleaner.
Cotton balls. Shampoo (all-purpose or conditioning). Slicker brush.
Comb. Blending shears.

Grooming Procedure
- Cut the nails by removing the tips only, and avoid cutting the quick.
  If the nail bleeds, apply styptic powder to stop the bleeding. Any
  rough nail edges may be removed with a file.
- Clean the ears with a liquid ear cleaner. Apply cleaner to a cotton
  ball and wipe all accumulated dirt and wax from the crevices of
  both ears.
- Bathe the dog in your shampoo of choice and rinse him
  thoroughly. Apply a conditioning rinse to help control static
  electricity.
- Towel dry the dog and finish drying him with a dryer while you
  brush the coat in the direction of its growth. This makes the hair
  dry smooth and straight.

82

- Comb through the entire coat to make sure all tangles are removed.
- With blending shears remove the hair that grows in between the toes on the top of the foot.
- Carefully scissor short the hair around the anus.

The completed long-haired Chihuahua should have a full ruff around the neck, with long hair on the ears to frame the face. The hair on the tail should be brushed into a full plume. This grooming should be done every 6 to 8 weeks.

CHIHUAHUA, SMOOTH COAT

Tools and Equipment

Nail cutter (scissor or guillotine). Styptic powder. Ear cleaner. Cotton balls. Shampoo (all-purpose or conditioning). Bristle brush. Rubber brush. Blending shears.

Grooming Procedure

- Cut the toenails by removing the tips only and avoiding the quick. If the nail should bleed, apply styptic powder to arrest the bleeding. Any rough nail edges may be smoothed with a file.
- Clean the ears with a liquid ear cleaner. Apply cleaner to a cotton ball and wipe all accumulated dirt and wax from all crevices in both ears.
- Bathe the dog in your shampoo of choice and rinse thoroughly. Apply a conditioning rinse if needed. A rubber brush may be used to lather the dog and remove excess dead coat.
- Towel dry the dog until damp and continue drying him in a cage with a dryer.
- With blending shears remove any stray hairs on the back of the thighs, on the back of the front legs, and on the sides of the neck. Enough hair should be removed only to give the dog a tidy appearance, never enough that it makes the dog look scissored.

The completed Chihuahua should have a clean outline, and the grooming should be done every 6 to 8 weeks.

CHOW CHOW

Tools and Equipment

Nail cutter (guillotine or scissor). Styptic powder. Ear cleaner. Cotton balls. Shampoo (conditioning or all-purpose). Slicker brush. Comb (wide-spaced). Straight scissors.

Grooming Procedure

- Cut the toenails by removing the tips only; avoid cutting the quick. If the nail should bleed, apply styptic powder to stop the bleeding. Any rough nail edges may be smoothed with a file.
- Clean the ears with a liquid cleaner. Apply the cleaner to a cotton ball and wipe all accumulated dirt and wax from the crevices of both ears.
- With the slicker brush, brush out the *entire* coat. As you brush, layer the coat so as to get down to the skin. This helps remove matting and bunching up of the coat.
- Bathe the dog with your shampoo of choice. Rinse thoroughly. A cream rinse may be applied to make easier the brushing out of the coat after the bath.

- Towel off the dog. A high velocity dryer may be used at this time to blow off excess water in the coat. Next, use a regular blow dryer while brushing out the coat with a slicker brush. Brush in the direction of hair growth. When the coat is completely dry, comb it through with a wide-spaced comb to check for any bunching of the coat.
- Carefully scissor the excess hair around the anus.
- Scissor the hair from underneath the paw and from between the foot pads, as well. Any hair that grows in between the toes and on the top of the feet should be scissored as well, to give a clean, neat appearance. The paws should appear compact and catlike.
- The whiskers and eyebrows may be removed with scissors if desired.
- Any excess hair on the back of the hocks should be removed.

This grooming should be done every 4 to 6 weeks.

Cocker Spaniel, American

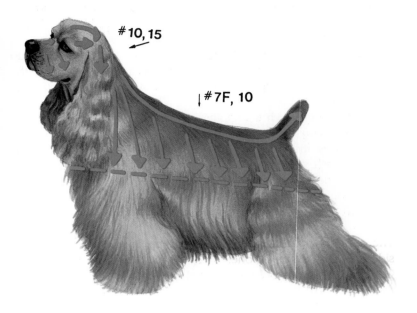

#10, 15

#7F, 10

Tools and Equipment

Slicker brush. Steel comb (¼" spaced teeth). Nail clipper. Stripping knife. Oster clipper. #10, #15, #5F, #7F, #8½ blades. Thinning shears. Scissors.

Grooming Procedure

- Brush the coat with a slicker brush. If the dog has mats under the elbows and inside the hind legs, shave them out with a #10 or #15 blade.
- Clean the ears.
- Wash the dog. Use protein shampoo and cream rinse. If the coat is matted, soak all mats well.
- Cage dry the dog until half dry. Finish drying on the table, blowing him dry while brushing and combing. Dry the shortest hair first. The dog should be completely combed out before clipping.
- Clip the face with a #10 blade against the grain on the jawbone and cheeks. Clean all hair off the lower jaw, including the creases of the lips. It is necessary to insert your finger into the corner of the mouth, pull the skin taut, and clip off all the hair. Use a #15 blade in this area. Pull down the chin flesh and clean off all hairs. This is very visible when the mouth is open. It is important to clean this off for hygienic reasons.

- Make a reverse V in the stop with a #10 blade. Clip the top of the nose and under the eyes.
- Trim the back of the head, starting slightly forward from where the ears set on, with a #10 blade and blend this gradually into the neck. If the hair over the eyes is very long, use a #5F or #7F to trim it. Thinning shears or straight scissors can be used to blend hair into the top of the head.
- Ears are clipped with a #10 or #15 blade. Hair is clipped either up or down to remove as much hair as possible, inside and outside the ear. One-third the length of the ear is removed, usually about 2½ inches down the ear.
- Go over the body with a stripping knife to determine whether the dog is shedding his undercoat. This will minimize clipper marks.
- Clip the body, including the tail, with a #7F. Clip *with* the direction of hair growth, gradually coming off the side and blending it into the longer hair. Do not make a straight line (hula skirt effect). The line can be dropped for a slimming effect on overweight dogs.
- Clean off the whole tail, top and bottom. Clip under the tail area, down about 2 to 3 inches, and blend into the feathering.
- The neck should be clipped with a #10 blade on the front and sides. Clip to the breastbone.
- Go over the neck and back with a stripping knife.
- Clip the nails at this time.
- Scissor the hair around the foot flush with the pads. Feel around to see if there are mats between the foot pads. If necessary, shave out any mats with a #15 blade.
- Cocker feet should be round. Use the dog's nails as a guide, lining up the scissor vertically against the nails, and then cut. Nails should not be seen. Sometimes it is necessary to lift the long leg coat just to see the front of the foot. Lift up the hair and make the first circle of the foot with scissors. Comb over and over, down and out. Keep correcting your circle.
- Uneven hair on the legs should be scissored to blend in and give a tidy look. Scissor the tips of the hair for a full-coated look, or remove 1 to 2 inches by scissoring for a "puppy cut."

ENGLISH COCKER SPANIEL

Tools and Equipment

Nail cutter (scissor or guillotine). Styptic powder. Ear cleaner. Cotton balls. Shampoo (all-purpose or conditioning). Slicker brush. Comb. Blending shears. Straight shears. Electric clipper. #7, #10, and #15 blades.

Grooming Procedure

- Nails should be cut by removing the tips only. Avoid cutting into the quick, although if the nail should bleed, apply styptic powder to stop the bleeding. Any rough nail edges may be smoothed with a file.
- Clean the ears by moistening a cotton ball with liquid ear cleaner and wiping accumulated dirt and wax from all crevices in both ears.
- Cut the hair under the paw and between the pads with a clipper and a #15 blade.
- Cut the hair on the abdomen from the groin to the navel with a #10 blade. Clip *with* the growth of hair.
- Brush out the entire dog to remove any matting and/or dead coat.
- Bathe the dog in your shampoo of choice and rinse him well. A conditioning cream rinse may be used to help cut down on static electricity and to make the coat more manageable.
- Towel dry the dog until he is damp, and then fluff dry with a dryer while brushing the coat in the direction of its growth. This helps the hair lie flat.
- With the #10 blade, clip the muzzle in the direction of hair growth and continue clipping over the cheek to the front of the ear opening. Clip the hair from the chin down to the throat. Continue to the top of the breastbone and inside the "V" of the throat seams (where the hair growing in two different directions comes together).
- The top of the skull should be clipped, starting about ½ inch behind the eyebrows to the back of the skull. The top ⅓ of each ear should be clipped on both the inner and outer side of the ear leather. The hair just in front of the ear opening should be carefully clipped, as well, to allow air to circulate in the ear canal.
- With a #7 blade, clip from just under the ear flap down the side of the neck to the shoulder.
- The top body coat may also be cut with the #7 blade. Start at the base of the skull and work to the tip of the tail. Clip from the spine down, over the sides of the dog, to just past the widest part of the rib cage. This line is almost straight across the side of the dog, except in the shoulder area where it goes down to where the front leg joins the body on the front side. On the back leg, the clipper

line goes a little lower to expose the muscle on the top of the outer thigh.

- An optional method for the top coat, and, actually, the more correct way, is to leave the coat natural but to thin it out. This helps it lie flat against the dog. The lines for this method are the same as for clipping the dog.
- The English Cocker should not be left with too much coat on the legs or abdomen. This hair should be shortened up with the blending shears so as to look natural.
- With blending shears, to give the foot a tight compact look, remove the hair growing out between the toes and on top of the feet.
- Again, with the blending shears, blend in the eyebrows to give the skull a long, lean look without a pronounced stop.

The completed English Cocker Spaniel should give the appearance of a short-bodied, strong-limbed dog with a distinctive head. This breed should be groomed every 6 to 8 weeks.

COLLIE, ROUGH COAT

Tools and Equipment

Slicker brush. Large pin brush. Pure boar bristle brush. Steel comb (fine/medium). Long hair molting comb (#565). Wood utility comb. Scissor. Thinning shear. Oster #10 blade. Ear cleaner. Medicated ear powder. Protein coat conditioner. High velocity dryer. Nail clipper. Tearless protein shampoo. Cotton balls. Oster A-5 clipper.

Grooming Procedure

- Spray the entire coat with protein coat conditioner. This adds body to the coat and helps repair split ends. Brush through the entire coat with a large pin brush, alternating with a slicker brush in matted areas and a molting comb as needed. Work layer by layer—alternating brush and comb—to remove mats and loose undercoat. Lift the coat up with your hand, working on thin layers at a time. Brush down and out until all mats and loose hair are removed. Work deep into the coat, but do not brush to the skin or you will cause abrasion. Start at the rear of the dog, at the bottom of the skirt area. Work through the entire coat until the outer coat is separated well and combs smoothly. Work vigorously. The more hair you remove now, the less hair you need to wash and dry.

- Comb through the entire coat with a wide-tooth utility comb. Use a fine steel comb on the soft hair behind the ears. With your fingers, strip out dead hair behind the ears.

- Swab the ears with a cotton ball that has been moistened with ear cleaner. This will remove the dirt and control ear odor. Follow this with a dry cotton ball and dust the ears with medicated ear powder.

- Cut the nails with a guillotine-type nail clipper. Nails should be cut monthly.

- Check between the foot pads and under the feet for burrs, tar, etc. Scissor the hair under the foot even with the pads. Trim any hair around the paw that touches the ground and neaten the entire foot. Trim the hair growing out from between the toes with thinning shears. The toes should lie close, like those on a cat's foot.

- Bathe the dog with a tearless protein shampoo that is pH-alkaline. This will add fullness and body to the coat and restructure damaged hair.

- Use a high velocity dryer to blow excess water off the dog while the dog is still in the tub. This will speed up the drying time and help prevent the coat from becoming overly dry. Cage dry until the hair is damp. Finish drying on the table, using a blow dryer and a pin brush to separate all the hair and remove all of the loose coat.

- Brush the entire coat and be sure to brush to the skin, using the

dryer to style and separate the hair. Follow by combing the entire coat.

- The whiskers may be removed with scissors to improve the expression (optional).
- Use a fine comb to finish the head and the ears. Comb straight back. Keep the muzzle smooth. The excess hair behind the ears may be thinned with a thinning shear.
- Comb out the leg feathering. Trim excess hair on the feet and hocks. The hind legs are to be smooth below the hock joint, with a perpendicular line from the hock to the ground. Leave feathering on the forelegs full, but trim it so that it naturally meets the pastern and does not touch the ground.
- Scissor any long hair under the tail that hangs over the anus. Be sure the anus is clear and then use a #10 blade to blend down under the tail area so it does not collect feces.
- Lightly mist the coat with protein coat conditioner to add brilliance and fragrance. Back brush the coat with the pin brush so the coat stands out away from the body.

COLLIE, SMOOTH COAT

Tools and Equipment

Slicker brush (gentle). Steel comb (medium/fine). Pure boar bristle brush. Short hair molting comb (#564). Scissor. Eye stain remover. Ear cleaner. Medicated ear powder. Protein coat conditioner. Tearless protein shampoo. Cotton balls. Nail clipper.

Grooming Procedure

- Spray the entire coat with protein coat conditioner. This adds body to the coat and helps repair split ends. Brush through the entire coat with the gentle slicker to remove loose or dead hair. Then, comb with the molting comb made for short-haired breeds (#564) to take out loose undercoat.
- Swab the ears with a cotton ball that has been moistened with ear cleaner. This will remove the dirt and control ear odor. Follow this with a dry cotton ball and dust the ears with medicated ear powder.
- Cut the nails with a guillotine-type nail clipper. Nails should be cut monthly.
- Bathe the dog with a tearless protein shampoo that is pH-alkaline. This will add fullness and body to the coat and at the same time restructure damaged hair.

- Use a high velocity dryer to blow excess water off the dog while the dog is still in the tub. This will speed up the drying time and help prevent the coat from becoming overly dry. Cage dry the dog until the hair is damp. Finish drying him on the table, using a blow dryer and a pin brush to separate all of the hair and remove all of the loose coat. Finish with a steel comb through the entire coat, paying special attention to the fine hair behind the ears. Use the fine side of the comb for this area.
- With a scissor, neaten the hair at the base and on the inside of the ear.
- Check between the foot pads and under the feet for burrs, tar, etc. Scissor the hair under the foot even with the pads. Trim any hair around the paw that touches the ground and neaten the entire foot. Use thinning shears to trim the hair growing out between the toes. Be sure to neaten the hair on the back of the rear pasterns.
- The whiskers may be removed with scissors to improve the expression (optional).
- Under the body should be natural, but remove all straggly hair with a thinning shear to create a smooth line.
- Use a thinning shear to give a nice rounded look to the rump. Never trim to excess or until noticeable. The coat should appear smooth but natural.
- Top brush the coat with a pure bristle brush that has been sprayed with protein coat conditioner. This adds brilliance and fragrance to the coat.

DACHSHUND, LONG COAT

Tools and Equipment
  Slicker brush. Metal comb (medium). Medicated ear powder. Nail clippers. Eye drops (eye stain remover). Scissors. Oster A-5 clipper. #10 blade. Cotton balls.

Grooming Procedure
- Brush the entire coat with the slicker brush, removing any mats with the metal comb.
- Clean the ears using medicated ear powder, and lightly pluck stray hairs from the insides.
- Clean the eyes by wiping with a cotton ball that has been moistened with eye drops. This will also help to remove any stains around the eyes.
- Cut the tips of the toenails with the nail clipper, being careful not to cut the quick.
- Using the #10 blade, shave the anal area, being certain not to put the blade in direct contact with the skin. (Note: Shaving this area is a decision to be left to the dog's owner.)
- Using the #10 blade, shave the stomach area from groin to naval and down the insides of the thighs. (Again, this depends on the dog owner's preferences.)
- With the scissors clip the whiskers from the muzzle, under the chin, the sides of the face, and above the eyes. (Whiskers should be clipped only if the dog's owner wants this done.)
- Put a cotton ball in each ear (this prevents water from entering the ear canal) and bathe the dog. Fluff dry him.
- Brush the coat with the slicker brush and comb with the metal comb, paying special attention to the feathering on the legs, tail, and ears.

Dachshund, Smooth Coat

Tools and Equipment

Sisal (natural bristle) brush. Medicated ear powder. Nail clipper. Eye drops (eye stain remover). Lanolin coat conditioner. Chamois cloth. Cotton balls. Scissors.

Grooming Procedure

- Brush the coat briskly with the sisal brush.
- Clean the ears using the medicated ear powder.
- Clean the eyes by wiping with a cotton ball that has been moistened with eye drops. This will also help remove any stains around the eyes.
- Clip the tips of the toenails with the nail clippers, being careful not to cut the quick.
- With the scissors clip the long whiskers from the muzzle, under the chin, from the sides of the face, and above the eyes. (Note: Clipping the whiskers is a decision to be left to the dog's owner.)
- Put a cotton ball in each ear (this prevents water from entering the ear canal) and bathe the dog. Cage dry him.
- Put a few drops of lanolin coat conditioner into the palms of your hands, rub together lightly, and gently massage into the coat.
- Brush the coat with the sisal brush to distribute the conditioner, and then lightly rub over the coat with a chamois cloth, thus giving it a nice sheen.

The smooth-coated Dachshund should be bathed every eight weeks. Between baths, the dog should be brushed regularly by the owner to help maintain a healthy, shiny coat. The ears should be checked weekly; the nails should be checked monthly and clipped if necessary.

Dachshund, Wire Coat

Tools and Equipment
Sisal (natural bristle) brush. Metal comb (medium). Toenail clipper. Medicated ear powder. Eye drops (eye stain remover). Oster A-5 clipper. #10 blade. Thinning shears. Scissors. Cotton balls.

Grooming Procedure
- Brush the coat thoroughly with the sisal brush.
- Comb through the coat to remove all loosened hair.
- Clean the ears, using the medicated ear powder, and lightly pluck any stray hair from the insides.
- Clean the eyes by wiping with cotton that has been moistened with eye stain remover.
- Cut the tips of the toenails with the toenail clipper, being careful not to cut the quick.
- With the #10 blade on the Oster clipper, shave the stomach from groin to navel and down the insides of the thighs.
- Shave the anal area, being certain not to put the blade in direct contact with the skin (½" each side).
- Put a cotton ball in each ear (this prevents water from entering the ear canal) and bathe the dog. Cage dry him.
- With the scissors, snip hair from between the pads and toes of the feet and around the edges for a neat effect.
- With scissors or thinning shears, trim straggly hairs from around the ankles on the front feet and from the hocks down to the feet on the hind legs.
- Comb the hair on the face downward and with scissors, or thinning shears, trim the lower edge evenly.
- With the scissors, or thinning shears, trim evenly the lower edge of the belly fringe.
- Comb through the coat and remove all loosened hair.

96

DALMATIAN

Tools and Equipment
Nail cutter (guillotine or scissor). Styptic powder. Ear cleaner. Cotton balls. Shampoo (all-purpose or whitening). Rubber brush. Hound glove. Spray conditioner or coat gloss. Straight scissor.

Grooming Procedure
- Nails should be cut by removing the tips only and avoiding the quick. If the nail should bleed, apply styptic powder to stop the bleeding. Any rough nail edges may be removed with a file.
- Clean the ears with a liquid cleaner. Apply the cleaner to a cotton ball and wipe all accumulated dirt and wax from all crevices in both ears.
- Bathe the dog in your choice of shampoo. Lather the dog, using the rubber brush to remove dead hair. Rinse him thoroughly.
- Towel dry the dog and complete the drying by placing him in a cage, to which a dryer has been attached.
- When the dog is completely dry, brush the coat with a hound brush to remove any remaining dead hair and to make the hair lie flat.
- Lightly spray the coat with a conditioner or coat gloss and buff with a clean dry cloth.
- The whiskers and eyebrows may be removed if desired.

DOBERMAN PINSCHER

Tools and Equipment
Nail cutter (scissor or guillotine). Styptic powder. Ear cleaner.
Cotton balls. Shampoo (all-purpose, dark coat, or conditioning).
Rubber brush. Blending shears. Straight shears. Spray conditioner.

Grooming Procedure
- Nails should be cut by removing tips only; avoid cutting the quick.
  If the nail bleeds, apply styptic powder to stop the bleeding. Any
  rough nail edges may be smoothed by filing.
- Clean the ears by moistening a cotton ball with liquid ear cleaner
  and wiping accumulated wax and dirt from all crevices in both ears.
- Bathe the dog by lathering with your shampoo of choice. Rinse him
  thoroughly. An after-bath conditioner or a hot oil treatment may be
  applied to the coat and then rinsed off. This helps control dandruff.
- Towel dry the dog and then place him in a cage with a dryer until
  he is completely dry.

- A rubber brush may be used to remove any dead, unwanted hair.
- Pet Dobermans generally do not need much trimming unless the owner specifies this. Areas to be trimmed are the edges of the ears, the ear opening, the whiskers, and the eyebrows. Any areas where there are seams (two different directions of hair growth come together) may be blended with blending shears. Any excess hair on the back of the front legs may be removed, as well as the hair on the back of the thighs. The sides of the neck may need attention also.
- To give the Doberman a final touch, a small amount of spray conditioner or coat gloss should be lightly misted over the coat. Then polish with a clean cloth or a hound brush.

The completed Doberman Pinscher should appear sleek with a crisp outline. This grooming should be done every 10 to 12 weeks.

ENGLISH SETTER

Tools and Equipment

Nail cutter (scissor or guillotine). Styptic powder. Ear cleaner. Cotton balls. Clipper with a #7, #10, and #15 blade. Shampoo (whitening or all-purpose). Slicker brush. Comb. Blending shears. Straight shears. Conditioning rinse.

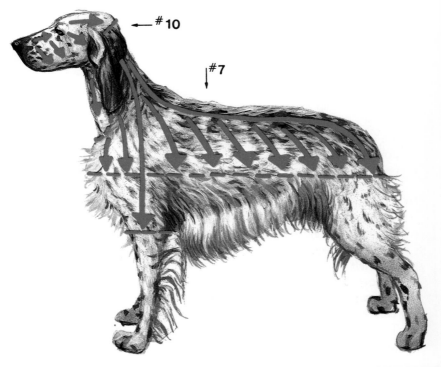

- Nails should be cut by removing the tips only and avoiding the quick. If the nail bleeds, apply styptic powder to stop the bleeding. Any rough nail edges may be smoothed out with a file.
- Clean the ears with a liquid ear cleaner. Apply this to a cotton ball and wipe accumulated wax and dirt from all crevices in both ears.
- With a #15 blade, cut the hair under the foot and between the pads. This hair may be scissored off instead, if desired.
- Cut the hair on the abdomen from groin to navel with a #10 blade, going *with* the growth of hair.
- Brush out the entire coat to remove dead hair and any mats that have formed.
- Bathe the dog in your shampoo of choice and rinse him thoroughly. After the bath, apply conditioner to the coat and rinse
- Towel dry the dog until he is damp and then fluff dry the rest of the way. Use a slicker brush to brush the hair while it is drying. While drying, always brush *with* the growth of the hair so that it lies flat. Continue until the dog is completely dry.
- With the #10 blade, clip the muzzle in the direction of hair growth and continue clipping over the cheeks to in front of the ear opening. Clip the hair on the chin and continue down the throat to the top of the breastbone, staying inside the "V" of the neck seams and clipping *with* the growth of hair. The top of the head may be clipped with the #10 also, or it may be smoothed out with blending shears.
- The ears should be clipped with the #10 blade about one-third of the way down from the top, where the ears join the skull. Leave some hair on the front edge of the ear to soften the expression.
- With a #7 blade, clip down the sides of the neck from under the ear to the shoulder.
- If the top body coat is thick, this area may also be clipped off with a #7 blade. Start at the base of the skull and continue to the root of the tail. Clip down over the sides of the ribcage to just below the widest part of the ribs. This line is almost straight across the side of the dog, except in the shoulder area where it slopes down to the point at which the front leg joins the body on the front side. On the back leg, the clipper line goes a little lower to expose the muscle on the top of the outer thigh.
- 11a. An optional method, and actually the correct way, would be to use a stripping knife and thinning shears to card out the back of the dog in order to make the hair lie smooth and flat naturally. The same lines would apply.
- The hair on top of the feet that grows between the toes should be removed to give a tidy, compact and well-knuckled look.
- Excessive hair on the back of the hocks should be removed.
- The tail should be trimmed into a triangular flag shape (plume). The tip should be long enough to just reach the hock.

ENGLISH SPRINGER SPANIEL

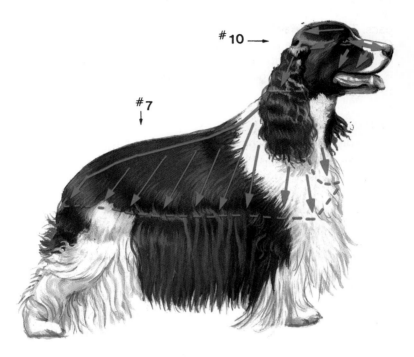

Tools and Equipment

Slicker brush. Short hair molting comb (#564). Pure boar bristle brush. Comb (fine/medium). Tearless protein shampoo. Scissor. Pin brush. Thinning shear. Ear cleaner. Medicated ear powder. Protein coat conditioner. High velocity dryer. Nail clipper. Cotton balls. Oster A-5 clipper. #10 blade. #7 blade.

Grooming Procedure

- Spray the entire coat with protein coat conditioner. This adds body to the coat and helps repair split ends. Comb through the entire coat with the molting comb; this will remove dead undercoat. Start at the rear of the dog, at the bottom of the skirt area. Work in sections, using your other hand to lift the hair ahead of the section you are working on. Work through the entire dog from the back to the neck area. Then brush through the coat with a slicker brush to remove the top dead coat. Work vigorously. The more hair you remove now, the less hair you need to wash and dry later.
- Swab the ears with a cotton ball that has been moistened with ear cleaner. This will remove the dirt and control ear odor. Follow this with a dry cotton ball and dust the ears with medicated ear powder.

101

- Cut the nails with a guillotine-type nail clipper. Nails should be cut monthly.
- Check between the foot pads and under the feet for burrs, tar, etc. With a #10 blade, clip the hair under the feet and between the pads.
- Bathe the dog with a tearless protein shampoo that is pH-alkaline. This will add fullness and body to the coat and restructure damaged hair.
- Use a high velocity dryer to blow excess water off the dog while the dog is still in the tub. This will speed up the drying time and help prevent the coat from becoming overly dry. Cage dry the dog until the hair is damp. Then, finish drying on the table, using a blow dryer and a pin brush to separate all the hair and remove all of the loose coat.
- Brush the entire coat and be sure to brush to the skin, using the dryer to style and separate the hair. Follow by combing the entire coat, using the fine side of the comb on the soft hair behind the ears.
- Use a #10 blade to clip the hair around the anus. Just clear the area and do not use heavy pressure. Scissor any long hair under the tail that hangs over the anal area and that may become soiled.
- Shave the stomach area with a #10 blade, going *with* the lay of the hair.
- Clip the head and muzzle, from above the brow to the base of the skull, with a #10 blade.
- Use the #10 blade to shave the cheek to the outer corner of the ear. Shave the folds in the lower jaw area—under the jaw and the throat to approximately one or two inches above the breastbone. Taper into the unclipped area of the apron. Make a deep "U" shape from ear to ear, always working *with* the grain of the hair. If you have trouble getting the flews of the lips clean, carefully stretch the skin and go lightly against the grain. The chest should be left full to accentuate the depth of the chest.
- Clip the front and back of the ears with a #10 blade about one-third of the way down the ear leather. Ear furnishings should be long: do not shorten! Just neaten uneven bottoms with scissors. The bottom edges of the ears should be curved, not square. (Note: one third refers to one-third of the overall ear, including the feathering.)
- Clip the body with a #7F blade. The body blades you use will vary, depending on the type of Springer coat and skin sensitivity. Clip from the base of the skull to the end of the tail (depending on coat texture, a #7F blade may be changed to a #7, #9, or #10). Clip both sides of the body, from the sides of the neck to the shoulder joint in the front leg and down to the thigh on the rear leg. Looking at the dog from the side, you should have blended from the front elbow up gradually to about one inch under the tail. Do not clip

below the area where the coat begins to hang down naturally. Follow the contour of the body, directing your clipper in the direction the hair grows. *Do not go against the grain or across the grain.* Lift your clipper slightly as you near the end of your clipped area, so as to blend the clipped area into the non-clipped area of the skirt and leg. It takes a slight twist of the wrist to accomplish this, as if you were using the end of the clipper as a shovel. You must work to blend the clipped area into the fringe area, leaving no uneven lines or ridges.

- Clip the tail with a #7F blade. Always clip *with* the grain—the way the hair grows—and never against the growth. To prevent irritation, use a very light pressure on the underside of the tail. Blend the area under the tail into the skirt.
- Use a thinning shear to shape the legs so that they appear even and tapered. Remove all straggly hair, and thin and shorten excess feathering—especially from the hocks to the feet.
- Use the thinning shear to blend in any uneven lines between shaved and unshaved areas.
- Feet should be neat, rounded, and blended into the legs.
- Top brush the coat with a pure bristle brush that has been sprayed with protein coat conditioner. This adds brilliance and fragrance.

FLAT-COATED RETRIEVER

Tools and Equipment

Nail cutter (guillotine or scissor). Styptic powder. Ear cleaner. Cotton balls. Shampoo (conditioning or all-purpose). Slicker brush. Comb. Straight shears. Blending shears.

Grooming Procedure

- Cut the nails by removing only the tips and by not cutting the quick. If the nail bleeds, apply styptic powder to stop the bleeding. Any rough nail edges may be smoothed with a file.
- Clean the ears with a liquid ear cleaner. Moisten a cotton ball with cleaner and wipe all accumulated wax and dirt from the crevices in both ears.

- Brush out the entire coat to remove any mats and/or dead coat.
- Bathe the dog in your shampoo of choice and rinse him thoroughly. A conditioning cream rinse may be used to help cut down on static electricity and to give the coat a shine.
- Towel dry the dog. Use a dryer to complete the drying process. While blow drying, brush the coat in the direction of its growth to make it lie smooth. After drying, comb through the coat to remove any tangles.
- With straight scissors cut the hair from the bottom of the foot, between the pads. Remove the hair on the outer edge of the foot by the pads to round the foot. With blending shears remove the hair that grows from between the toes and on the top of the feet.
- The hair directly under the ear flap may be thinned out to allow the ear to lie close to the skull. The edge of the ear may be neatened with the blending shears.
- Excess hair on the back of the hock should be neatened.
- The tail may be neatened. It should be carried straight out as a smooth extension of the topline. At rest, the tip of the tail should reach the hock joint, but not any further.

This breed should not be overly groomed but should maintain a natural appearance. Grooming should be done every 8 to 12 weeks.

Fox Terrier, smooth

Tools and Equipment

Pure boar bristle brush. Ear cleaner. Medicated ear powder. Nail clipper. Scissor. Thinning shear. Stripping knife, fine. Mink oil. Tearless protein shampoo. Rubber curry brush. Cotton balls.

Grooming Procedure

- Brush the entire coat with a pure boar bristle brush, followed with a rubber curry brush.
- Swab the ears with a cotton ball that has been moistened with ear cleaner. This will remove dirt and control ear odor. Follow with a dry cotton ball and dust the ears with medicated ear powder.
- Cut the nails with a guillotine-type nail clipper. Nails should be cut monthly.
- Check between the foot pads and under the feet for burrs, tar, etc.
- Bathe the dog with a tearless protein shampoo that is pH-alkaline. This will add body to the coat and restructure damaged hair.
- Cage dry until damp. Finish drying on the table, using a blow dryer and a pure bristle brush.
- The whiskers may be removed with a scissor to improve expression, although this is optional.

- Trim with a scissor any stray hair on the edges of the ears.
- Smooth any hair that detracts from an overall sleek look. Use a fine stripping knife to remove rough ridges and to get the coat to lie close to the skin.
- Trim any hair around the paw that looks long. The foot should be compact and neat.
- Finish with a mist of mink oil to create a brilliant shine, and brush this in with a pure bristle brush.

Fox Terrier, wire

Tools and Equipment

Slicker brush. Metal Comb (medium). Medicated ear powder. Toenail clipper. Eye drops (eye stain remover). Cotton balls. Oster A-5 clipper. Scissors. Thinning shears. #10 blade. #8½ or #7 or #5 blade.

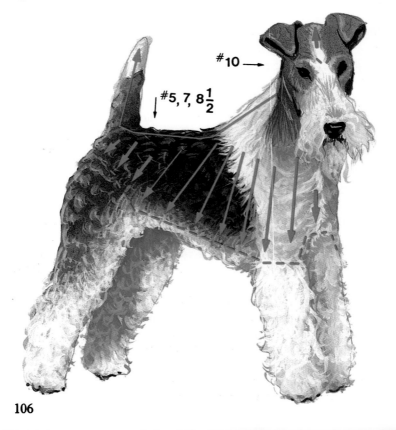

Grooming Procedure

- Brush the entire coat and tail with the slicker brush. Comb through with the metal comb, paying special attention to any tangles.
- Clean the ears using the medicated ear powder, and lightly pluck any stray hair from inside the ears.
- Clean the eyes by wiping with cotton that has been moistened with eye drops. Use the same product to remove any stains under or around the eyes.
- Cut the tips of the toenails with the toenail clipper, being especially careful not to cut the quick.
- With the #10 blade on the Oster clipper, shave the anal area, being certain not to put the blade in direct contact with the skin (½" each side).
- Shave the stomach area from groin to navel and down the insides of the thighs.
- With the #10 blade shave the head, starting at the center of the eyebrows and working back to the base of the skull. Then shave from the center again to the outer corners of the eyes. This line should be about ¾" above the inner corner of the eye and it should taper into the outer corner, thus making a triangle. Next shave down from the outer corners of the eyes, to within ¾" from the corners of the mouth, and continue this line across and under the chin.
- Shave both sides of the ears, and from the back edges of the ears shave down diagonally to a point at the base of the throat, thus forming a "V" shape.
- With the #8½, #7, or #5 blade on the Oster A-5 clipper (according to the length of the coat desired), start at the base of the skull and clip down the back to the base of the tail.
- Clip the top half of the tail and blend down either side of the bottom fringe. Comb the fringe downward and scissor the lower edge, making a close feather shape.
- With the clipper, clip down the sides of the neck to the shoulder and then down to the elbow.
- Clip down the chest to the breastbone and slope the pattern down diagonally to the center front of the legs.
- From the first clip down the back, clip down the sides of the stomach, arching the pattern over the hips. (From the side, the pattern line should slope down diagonally from the breastbone, straight across the tops of the front legs, sloping up across the stomach, arching up over the hips and down to a point in the rear.)
- Comb through the coat to remove all loosened hair.
- Put a cotton ball in each ear (this prevents water from entering the ear canal) and bathe the dog. Cage dry him.
- Brush and comb through the coat.

- Using the same blade on the Oster A-5 clipper as before, repeat the process for the pattern, blending the hair down from the pattern with the blade.
- Scissor around the edges of the ears.
- Comb the eyebrows forward and scissor a "V" in the center.
- Comb the hair on the face and eyebrows forward and downward. Align the base of your scissors at the nose and the tip of the scissors at the outer corner of the eye. Scissor the eyebrows from this angle, thus making a deep triangle, and be careful not to cut any hair from the top of the muzzle.
- Lightly scissor any stray hairs from around the edges and sides of the beard. Use thinning shears to shape the beard, which should be long and barrel-shaped.
- Use thinning shears to trim any stray hairs from the top of the muzzle.
- With the scissors, snip the hair from between the pads of the feet; while the dog is standing, scissor around the edges to give a neat effect (doing this first will give you a guide for shaping the legs).
- Scissor the front legs into straight tubular shapes.
- Scissor evenly the bottom of the chest fringe.
- Scissor the bottom of the belly fringe, following the contour of the dog's body and tapering up from the elbows on the front legs to the flanks at the rear.
- Scissor the hind legs, following the natural contours. From the back view, the legs should be straight on the outside edges; on the inside edges, the legs should be straight, up to the thighs, and then they should arch up and into the shave line.
- Lightly comb through the legs, fringe areas, and face, removing all excess hair and trimming any stray hairs as necessary.

The wire Fox Terrier should be groomed every 6 to 8 weeks. The ears should be checked weekly and cleaned if necessary, and the toenails should be checked and cut at the grooming session.

FRENCH BULLDOG

Tools and Equipment

Nail cutter (guillotine or scissor). Styptic powder. Ear cleaner. Cotton balls. Shampoo (all-purpose or whitening). Rubber brush. Hound glove. Straight scissors (small).

Grooming Procedure

- Cut the nails by removing only the tips and avoiding the quick. If the nail should bleed, apply styptic powder to stop the bleeding. Any rough nail edges may be smoothed with a file.
- Ears should be cleaned with a liquid cleaner. Apply the cleaner to a cotton ball and wipe all accumulated dirt and wax from all crevices in both ears.
- Bathe the dog in your shampoo of choice. Lather the dog, using the rubber brush to remove any dead coat. Special attention should be paid to the folds in the skin and around the eyes. Rinse the dog thoroughly.
- Towel dry the dog and complete the drying with a blow dryer. The French Bulldog may also be cage dried.
- When the dog is completely dry, brush the coat with a hound brush to remove dead coat and make the hair lie smooth.
- With straight scissors, scissor the hair around the edges of the ears. The whiskers and eyebrows may be removed if desired.

The French Bulldog should be groomed every 8 to 12 weeks.

GERMAN SHEPHERD DOG

Tools and Equipment
Slicker brush. Shedding blade. Metal rake (wide-tooth). Medicated ear powder. Eye drops (eye stain remover). Cotton balls. Scissors. Metal comb (wide-tooth). Toenail clipper, large.

Grooming Procedure
- Starting at the head, brush the entire coat and tail with the slicker brush.
- During the shedding season, use the shedding blade (work from the rear to the front) and remove any mats in the undercoat (*i.e.,* neck, chest, thighs) with the metal rake.
- Clean the ears, using medicated ear powder, and lightly pluck any stray hair from the insides of the ears.
- Clean the eyes by wiping with cotton that has been moistened with eye drops. This will also help to remove any stains around the eyes.
- Cut the tips of the toenails with the large toenail clipper, being careful not to cut the quick.

- With the scissors, clip the whiskers from the muzzle, chin, sides of the face, and above the eyes. (Note: Clipping the whiskers is a decision to be left to the dog's owner.)
- Putting a cotton ball in each ear will prevent water from entering the ear canal. After doing this, bathe the dog and cage dry him.
- Brush through the coat briskly with the slicker brush, and then comb through with the metal comb to remove the loosened hair.
- With the scissors, snip the hair from between the pads and toes on the feet to give a neat appearance.

The German Shepherd Dog should be groomed every 8 or 10 weeks. Regular brushing with the slicker brush, by the owner, will help to keep the undercoat free of tangles. The ears should be checked weekly and cleaned if necessary, and the toenails should be checked and cut at the grooming session.

GERMAN SHORTHAIRED POINTER

Tools and Equipment
   Nail cutter (guillotine or scissor). Styptic powder. Ear cleaner.
   Cotton balls. Shampoo (all-purpose). Rubber brush. Hound glove.
   Spray conditioner or coat gloss.

Grooming Procedure
- Nails should be cut by removing only the tips to avoid cutting the
  quick. If the nail should bleed, apply styptic powder to stop the
  bleeding. Any rough edges may be smoothed with a file.
- Clean the ears by applying liquid cleaner to a cotton ball and wiping
  all accumulated wax and dirt from all crevices in both ears.
- Bathe the dog in your shampoo of choice. Lather the dog well,
  using a rubber brush to remove dead hair and dirt. Rinse the dog
  thoroughly.
- Towel dry the dog. Complete the drying with a cage dryer.
- When the dog is fully dry, brush the coat with a soft bristle brush
  or a hound glove to remove any remaining dead hair. This also
  makes the coat lie smooth.
- Lightly spray the coat with a conditioner or coat gloss and buff with
  a dry clean cloth.

The German Shorthaired Pointer should be groomed every 12
weeks.

German Wirehaired
Pointer

Tools and Equipment
   Nail cutter (guillotine or scissor). Styptic powder. Ear cleaner.
   Cotton balls. Shampoo (all-purpose or texturizing). Slicker brush.
   Comb. Stripping knife or a clipper with a #7 blade. Straight scissor.

Grooming Procedure
- Nails should be cut by removing only the tips and avoiding the
  quick. If the nail should bleed, apply styptic powder to stop the
  bleeding. Any rough nail edges may be removed with a file.
- Ears should be cleaned with a liquid cleaner. Apply the cleaner to
  a cotton ball and wipe all accumulated wax and dirt from all
  crevices in both ears.
- Brush through the entire coat to remove dead coat and
  accumulated dirt.

112

- The coat should be plucked, with the help of a stripping knife, to a length of about 1½ inches. The coat on the cheeks, ears, and top of the head should be plucked closer than 1½ inches in order to give a smooth appearance. A beard should be left, as well as eyebrows, which should be longer at the inside corner of the eye and taper to the outer corner. Any long hairs on the body should be plucked, with the neck and shoulder areas being slightly shorter than the back area so as to accentuate the length of the neck. Any long hairs on the legs should be removed, except for some feathering on the back of the front legs. For a shorter pet clip, use a clipper with a #7 blade to cut the hair from the top of the head, the cheeks, and the ears. Continue down the throat and neck, over the back, and down to the tail. Clip the sides down over the ribs, leaving some hair at the bottom of the ribcage to accentuate depth of chest. All clipper lines should be feathered off or blended so that no line between the clipped and non-clipped areas may be detected. The top and bottom of the tail may be clipped as well.
- The hair between the foot pads should be cut short with a straight scissor. The hair from the top of the foot that grows between the toes also should be cut short.
- Bathe the dog in your shampoo of choice.
- Towel dry the dog untill damp. Brush the coat flat *with* the direction of hair growth. Let the dog air dry if it is warm enough; otherwise, finish drying him in a cage dryer.
- When the dog is dry, go over the coat and remove any hairs that are sticking out. The German Shorthaired Pointer should have a clean outline and be groomed every 8 to 12 weeks.

Golden Retriever

Tools and Equipment
Nail cutter (guillotine or scissor). Styptic powder. Ear cleaner. Cotton balls. Shampoo (conditioning or all-purpose). Slicker brush. Comb. Straight scissors. Blending shears.

Grooming Procedure
- Nails should be cut by removing only the tips; avoid cutting into the quick. If the nail bleeds, apply styptic powder to stop the bleeding. Any rough nail edges may be smoothed with a file.
- Clean the ears with a liquid cleaner. Apply the cleaner to a cotton ball and wipe all accumulated dirt and wax from the crevices in both ears.
- To remove dead coat and any matted hair, brush out the entire dog with a slicker brush.
- Bathe the dog in your shampoo of choice and rinse him thoroughly. A conditioning rinse may be used to help cut down on static electricity.
- Towel dry the dog. Use a dryer to complete the drying as you brush the coat in the direction of its growth. After drying, comb through the coat to remove any tangles that remain.
- With straight scissors remove the hair on the bottom of the foot and between the pads. Remove the hair on the outer edge and underside of the paw to round the foot. With blending shears

remove the hair that grows out between the toes on the top side of the foot. The foot should have a round, well-knuckled–up, compact look.

- Excessive hair should be removed from the back of the hock to even up the hairs.
- The hair directly under the flap may be thinned out to allow the ear to hang close to the side of the head. The edge of the ear may be neatened up with the blending shears.
- The Golden's plume-like tail, when extended to the hock joint, should not exceed it. The tail should be trimmed so that it just touches the hock.
- Any hair around the anus may be carefully trimmed away.

The completed Golden Retriever should have a neat outline without looking scissored. This breed should be natural looking, and the grooming should be done every 6 to 8 weeks.

GREAT DANE

Tools and Equipment

Sisal (natural bristle brush). Medicated ear powder. Large nail clipper. Scissors. Eye drops (eye stain remover). Lanolin coat conditioner. Chamois cloth. Vitamin E oil. Cotton balls.

Grooming Procedure

- Brush the coat briskly with the sisal brush.
- Clean the ears using medicated ear powder.
- Clean the eyes by wiping with cotton that has been moistened with eye drops. This will also help to remove any stains around or under the eyes.
- Cut the tips of the toenails with the nail clipper, being careful not to cut the quick.
- With a damp cotton ball, gently wipe the insides of the lips, being certain to remove any trapped food particles.
- With the scissors, clip the whiskers from the muzzle, under the chin, the sides of the face, and above the eyes. (Note: Clipping the whiskers is a decision to be left to the dog's owner.)
- Place a cotton ball in each ear (this prevents water from entering the ear canal) and bathe the dog, paying special attention to the white areas (if the dog is a harlequin). Cage dry.
- Put a few drops of lanolin coat conditioner into the palms of your hands, rub together lightly, and gently massage this into the coat. Use more as necessary.
- Lightly brush the coat with the sisal brush to distribute the conditioner and then rub over the coat with the chamois cloth to give it a nice sheen.
- These large dogs tend to have bald, sometimes sore, patches on their elbows, pasterns, and hock joints. In this case, massage these patches with Vitamin E oil to heal them.

The Great Dane rarely needs bathing (every 3 or 4 months), but regular brushing with a sisal brush, by the owner, and a monthly application of lanolin coat conditioner will help maintain a healthy, shiny coat. The ears should be checked weekly, and the nails should be checked monthly. Clip the nails if necessary.

GREYHOUND

Tools and Equipment

Pure boar bristle brush. Sisal hound glove. Ear cleaner. Medicated ear powder. Nail clipper (extra large). Cotton balls. Mink oil spray. Tearless shampoo or whitening shampoo. Scissor. Thinning shear. Skin cream.

Grooming Procedure

- Brush the coat with a pure bristle brush. Follow with a thorough brushing, using the hound glove.
- Swab the ears with a cotton ball that has been moistened with ear cleaner. This will remove dirt and control ear odor. Follow with a dry cotton ball and dust the ears with medicated ear powder.
- Cut the nails with a guillotine-type nail trimmer. Nails should be cut monthly.
- Check between the foot pads and under the feet for burrs, tar, etc.
- Bathe the dog with a tearless shampoo that is balanced pH-alkaline. Use a tearless whitening shampoo for Greyhounds that are white or partially white.
- Cage dry till damp. Finish drying on the table, using a blow dryer and a pure bristle brush.
- The whiskers may be removed with a scissor to improve expression (optional).
- With a thinning shear, remove any straggly hair on the brisket, the sides of the neck, the backs of the thighs, in the rear tuck-up, or on the face.
- Calluses on the elbows can be rubbed with skin cream to soften and heal them.
- Finish with a mist of mink oil to create a brilliant shine and brush this in with a pure bristle brush.

117

Irish Setter

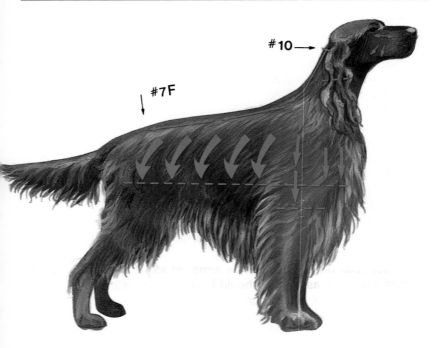

#10 →

#7F

Tools and Equipment

Slicker brush. Pure boar bristle brush. Pin brush, large. Nail clipper (extra-large). Ear cleaner. Medicated ear powder. Protein coat conditioner. High velocity dryer. Stripping knife. Molting comb for long hair. Oster A-5 clipper. #7F, #10 blades. Tearless protein shampoo. Cotton balls. Steel comb (medium/fine). Thinning shear. Scissor.

Grooming Procedure

- Spray the entire coat with protein coat conditioner. This adds body to the coat and helps repair split ends. Brush through the entire coat with the pin brush. Then, comb with the molting comb to take out loose, dead undercoat. Use the slicker brush to loosen up matted areas.
- Swab the ears with a cotton ball that has been moistened with ear cleaner. This will remove the dirt and control ear odor. Follow this with a dry cotton ball and dust the ears with medicated ear powder.
- Cut the nails with a guillotine-type nail trimmer. Nails should be cut monthly.
- Check between the foot pads and under the feet for burrs, tar, etc. Scissor the hair under the feet to prevent debris from adhering.

118

Trim any hair around the paw that touches the ground. *Do not take out any hair between the toes.*

- Scissor any long hair under the tail that hangs over the anus. Be sure the anus is clear, and then trim down under the tail area so it does not become soiled.
- The whiskers may be removed with scissors to improve the expression (optional).
- Bathe the dog with a tearless protein shampoo that is pH-alkaline. This will add fullness and body to the coat and restructure damaged hair.
- Use a high velocity dryer to blow excess water off the dog while the dog is still in the tub. This will speed up the drying time and help prevent the coat from becoming overly dry. Cage dry the dog until the hair is damp. Then finish drying on the table, using a blow dryer and a pin brush to separate all the hair and remove all of the loose coat.
- It is especially important that feathering on the legs, tail, and ears be blown dry to straighten and give a long-styled look. As you are drying, use the fine side of your steel comb to separate all hair and give a luxurious blown-dry look.
- Excess hair on the face can be removed with a #10 blade, going *with* the grain, as the jaw should have a clean outline.
- With the #7F blade, clip under the chin and down the throat to about 2" above the breastbone. As you near the end of your clipped area, lift the clipper slightly to blend the clipped into the non-clipped area of the chest. This takes a slight twist of the wrist, as if you were using the end of the clipper as a shovel. You must work to blend the clipped area into the fringe area, leaving no uneven lines or ridges. How far down you clip depends on how long you wish the neck to appear. Always cut *with* the lay of the hair, never against or across the grain. Work gradually to ensure that you don't remove too much coat.
- Clean out the hair around and under the ears. With a twist of the wrist action, blend the sides of the neck where the shaved area stops. Keep this shaved area under the ears and under the neck. *Do not use clippers on the topside of the neck.* The neck is to look long and lean, without throatiness. Use a thinning shear to blend the shaved area into the long area. *Always use thinning shears in combination with a comb.* Hold thinning shears pointed in the direction the hair grows; thin and comb to achieve the desired look. *Never cut across the grain.*
- The Irish Setter should have a clean appearance, so straggly hair can be removed with a stripping knife. Do not use clippers on the head.
- Holding the ear leather near the bottom, stretch it; and with a #10 blade, clip the ear one-third of the way down in the direction of hair

119

growth to give the appearance of a low-set ear. Do not trim the fold along the front edge of the ear. Trim into the *underside* of the fold only. Shave the underside of the ear one-third of the way down, also including the burr at the front. To remove as much hair as possible, you may go *against* the grain in this area. The shaved area inside the ear must be down as far as the shaved area on the outside of the ear. Trim the front edge of the upper ear with a scissor, blending the short hair into the longer hair. If the feathering on the inside of the ear is profuse, blend it down to give the appearance of ears being carried close to the head. Ears are to be long, and bottoms should be scissored only if they are uneven or straggly.

- If the shoulders have profuse hair, use thinning shears to create a smooth line with the neck gradually widening into the shoulders.
- The chest hair should be as long as possible and should only be shortened if it is uneven or straggly.
- Side hair and underbody hair should also be long and natural. Trim and shorten only if straggly or to achieve a natural contour from chest to tuck-up.
- Feathering on the back legs and under the tail should be combed down; only straggly hair should be removed. The back feet should be trimmed to achieve a rounded foot, catlike in shape, with plenty of hair between the toes. Use thinning shears to trim off excess rough hair or protruding hair between the toes that does not conform to the desired round shape. The back of the hock can be thinned to eliminate any bushiness, but it should not look scissored.
- Tail feathering should be long and combed down. For hygienic reasons, be sure that any profuse hair on the underside of the tail (hair that hangs over the anus) is removed. Straggly hair on the topside of the tail should be removed with thinning shears. Taper the tail so that it is wide at the base and narrows at the tip. Remove excess hair from the tail tip if it touches the ground; this will give the tail the proper length to balance the rest of the dog.
- Trim the front feet as you did the rear feet, but comb out the feathering and trim it to achieve a natural straight line that blends into the pastern.
- Lightly spray the coat with protein coat conditioner to add brilliance and fragrance; brush with a pure bristle brush.

Italian Greyhound

Tools and Equipment
Pure boar bristle brush. Ear cleaner. Medicated ear powder. Nail clipper. Scissor. Thinning shear. Mink oil spray. Tearless protein shampoo. Rubber curry brush. Cotton balls. Stripping knife, fine.

Grooming Procedure
- Brush the coat with a pure boar bristle brush, followed by a rubber curry brush.
- Swab the ears with a cotton ball that has been moistened with ear cleaner. This will remove dirt and control ear odor. Follow with a dry cotton ball and dust the ears with medicated ear powder.
- Cut the nails with a guillotine-type nail trimmer. Nails should be cut monthly.
- Check between the foot pads and under the feet for burrs, tar, etc.
- Bathe the dog with a tearless protein shampoo that is pH-alkaline. This will add body to the coat and restructure damaged hair.

- Cage dry untill damp. Finish drying on the table, using a blow dryer and a pure bristle brush.
- The whiskers may be removed with a scissor to improve expression (optional).
- Trim with a scissor any stray hair on or in the ears.
- Smooth any hair that detracts from an overall sleek look. Use a fine stripping knife to remove any long hair on the underside of the tail.
- Use thinning shears to trim any hair between the toes that looks long. The foot should be compact and neat.
- Finish with a mist of mink oil to create a brilliant shine, and brush this in with a pure bristle brush.

KEESHOND

Tools and Equipment

Slicker brush (large). Steel comb (fine/medium). Protein coat conditioner. High velocity dryer. Long hair molting comb (#565). Scissor. Pin brush (large). Nail clipper (extra large). Ear cleaner. Medicated ear powder. #10 blade. Tearless protein shampoo. Cotton balls. Thinning shear. A-5 clipper.

Grooming Procedure

- Spray the entire coat with protein coat conditioner. This adds body to the coat and helps repair split ends. Brush through the entire coat with a large pin brush, alternating with a slicker brush in matted areas. Start at the rear of the dog, at the bottom of the skirt area. Work in sections, using your other hand to lift the hair ahead of the section you are working on. Work layer by layer, working on thin layers at a time. Brush down and out until all mats and loose hair are removed. Work deep into the coat, but do not brush to the skin or you will cause abrasions. Work through the entire coat until the outer coat is well separated.

- If there is heavy matting around the reproductive organs or in the armpits on the front legs, use a #10 blade to carefully remove the mats, as brushing these areas can be uncomfortable for the dog. As you use the clipper, lift the coat out of the way so that when it is put back in place, the "shaved-out" areas will not be visible.
- Then comb through the entire coat with the long-hair molting comb. Work vigorously. The more hair you remove now, the less hair you will need to wash and dry.
- Comb the finer hair behind the ears with a fine steel comb.
- Swab the ears with a cotton ball that has been moistened with ear cleaner. This will remove the dirt and control ear odor. Follow this with a dry cotton ball and dust the ears with medicated ear powder.
- Cut the nails with a guillotine-type nail trimmer. Nails should be cut monthly.
- Bathe the dog with a tearless protein shampoo that is pH-alkaline. This will add fullness and body to the coat and restructure damaged hair.
- Use a high velocity dryer to blow excess water off the dog while he is still in the tub. This will speed up the drying time and help prevent the coat from becoming overly dry. Cage dry the dog until the hair is damp. Then finish drying on the table, using a blow dryer and a pin brush to separate all the hair and remove all of the loose coat.
- Follow by combing through the entire coat with a steel comb, paying special attention to the fine hair behind the ears. Use the fine side of the comb for this area.
- Scissor any long hair under the tail that hangs over the anus. Be sure the anus is clear. Use a #10 blade down under the tail so it does not collect feces.
- Check between the foot pads and under the feet for burrs, tar, etc. Scissor the hair under the foot even with the pads. With thinning shears, trim the hair growing out between the toes.
- Comb out the leg feathering and neaten. The hind legs should be smooth below the hock joint and perpendicular from hock to ground. Leave full the feathering on the fore legs but trim it so that it meets the pastern naturally and does not touch the ground.
- Back brush the entire coat with the pin brush so the coat stands out and away from the body.
- The whiskers may be removed with a scissor to improve expression, but this is optional.
- Lightly mist the coat with protein coat conditioner to add brilliance and fragrance.

KERRY BLUE TERRIER

#10 →

#7F

Tools and Equipment

Slicker brush. Long hair molting comb, #565. Pure boar bristle brush. Comb (fine/medium). Tearless protein shampoo. Scissor. Pin brush. Thinning shear. Ear forceps. Ear cleaner. Medicated ear powder. Coat gloss. Protein coat conditioner. High velocity dryer. Nail clipper (extra large). Cotton balls. Oster A-5 clipper. #10 blade. #7F blade.

Grooming Procedure

• Spray the entire coat with protein coat conditioner. This adds body to the coat and helps repair split ends. Brush through the entire coat with the slicker brush. Then comb thoroughly with the molting comb to remove dead undercoat. Start at the rear of the dog, at the bottom of the skirt area. Work in sections through the entire dog from the back to the neck area. Work vigorously. The more hair you remove now, the less hair you need to wash and dry.

- Swab the ears with a cotton ball that has been moistened with ear cleaner. This will remove dirt and control ear odor. Follow with a dry cotton ball and dust the ears with medicated ear powder. With your fingers or ear forceps, pluck hair inside the ears.
- Cut the nails with a guillotine-type nail trimmer. Nails should be cut monthly.
- Check between the foot pads and under the feet for burrs, tar, etc. Clip the hair under the feet and between the pads with a #10 blade.
- Bathe the dog in a tearless protein shampoo that is pH-alkaline. This will add fullness and body to the coat and restructure damaged hair.
- Use a high velocity dryer to blow excess water off the dog while the dog is still in the tub. This will speed up the drying time and help prevent the coat from becoming overly dry. Cage dry the dog until the hair is damp. Mist with coat gloss. Then finish drying on the table, using a blow dryer and a pin brush to separate all the hair and remove all of the loose coat.
- Comb the entire coat to the skin, using the medium part of the comb to separate all hair.
- Use a #10 blade to clip the hair around the anus. Just clear the area and do not use heavy pressure.
- Shave the abdomen with a #10 blade, going *with* the lay of the hair.
- Shave the ear with a #10 blade on both sides. Shave from the base to the tip. Then trim the outside edge of the ear, using your thumb as a protective guide to prevent nicks.
- Clip the top of the skull with a #10 blade, starting behind the eye socket and continuing back to the base of the skull. Leave plenty of eyebrow. Clip the side of the face, making a line from the outside corner of the eye to the mouth. Do not trim between the eyebrows or trim any part of the muzzle or under the eyes.
- Picking up the beard, clip under the jaw with the #10 blade. Leave a heavy beard, but clean out under the beard.

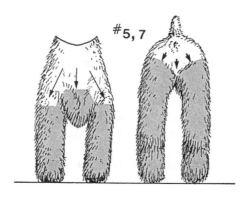

#5, 7

- Clip the throat with the #10 blade, forming a U from ear to ear, and shave down to one or two inches above the breastbone.
- Clip the body with a #7F blade. Body blades change, depending on the dog's type of coat and skin sensitivity. Clip from the base of the skull to the end of the tail (depending on coat texture, the 7F may be changed to a #7, #5, or #5F). Clip both sides of the body, from the sides of the neck to where the legs join the body in the front. Clip down to the thighs on the rear legs. In profile, there should be an even incline from elbow to hip. Follow the contour of the body, directing your clipper in the direction the hair grows. *Do not go against the grain or across the grain.* Lift the clipper slightly as you near the end of the skirt and leg. To accomplish this, it takes a slight twist of the wrist, as if you were using the end of the clipper as a shovel. You must work to blend the clipped area into the fringe area, leaving no uneven lines or ridges.
- Clip the tail with a #7F blade. Always clip *with* the grain—the way the hair grows—and never against the growth. To prevent irritation, use a very light pressure on the underside of the tail. Blend the area under the tail quite close.
- With the #7F blade clip the front of the dog's chest straight down the brisket, leaving a fringe between the front legs to define chest depth.
- With the slicker, brush the hair on the front legs up and then down. Comb through with the medium side of the comb. Lift the foot and shake the leg to allow the hair to fall naturally. Scissor the leg into a cylindrical shape. Use thinning shears to blend in any uneven line that you may have between the shaved area and unshaved area. Blend into the shoulder to create a straight line from shoulder to foot. Shape the foot so that it appears round and compact, but don't expose the toenails.
- Scissor evenly the furnishings on the sides of the body, making them fuller underneath the ribs and chest. Trim evenly the line from brisket to groin, striving for a natural tuck-up.
- Brush the rear leg up and then down, comb, and shake free. Blend the hip area into the rear leg using scissors. The rear leg should show good angulation and should be trimmed evenly to the middle of the thigh. From thigh to hock, remove straggly hair only. Trim evenly the backline of the hock. Round the foot and blend it into the leg. The inside of the back legs should form an arch.
- Comb the eyebrows forward, and with scissors pointing toward the nose, trim the hair beside the eyes to make them visible. Leave the fall (a fringe or shock of hair on top of the head) full between the eyebrows.
- Comb the beard forward and trim any straggly or extra-long whiskers to give a neat appearance.
- Top brush the coat with a pure bristle brush that has been sprayed with protein coat conditioner. This adds brilliance and fragrance.

126

LABRADOR RETRIEVER

Tools and Equipment

Nail clipper (guillotine or scissor). Styptic powder. Ear cleaner. Cotton balls. Shampoo (all-purpose or conditioning). Slicker brush. Blending shears. Spray coat gloss.

Grooming Procedure

- Nails should be cut by removing only the tips; avoid cutting the quick. If the nail bleeds, apply styptic powder to stop the bleeding. Any rough nail edges may be smoothed with a file.
- Clean the ears with a liquid cleaner. Apply the cleaner to a cotton ball and wipe all accumulated wax and dirt from all crevices.
- Brush out the entire coat to remove any dead hair.
- Bathe the dog in your shampoo of choice. Rinse thoroughly.
- Towel dry the dog until damp and finish drying him in a cage dryer.
- This breed needs little finishing if any at all. The tail may be trimmed to a blunt point, to accentuate the "otter-like" tail that this breed sports.
- A light misting with a coat conditioner or coat gloss may be applied and buffed until shiny. This is especially useful on black or chocolate Labs.
- The whiskers may be removed if desired.

Lhasa Apso

Tools and Equipment

Slicker brush. Matting comb. Metal combs (medium/fine). Medicated ear powder. Nail clipper. Oster A-5 clipper. #10 blade. Rubber bands. Cotton balls. Scissors.

Grooming Procedure

- Brush the entire coat and tail with the slicker brush, removing any mats with the matting comb. Comb through the coat, using the medium-toothed metal comb.
- Clean the ears, using the medicated ear powder, and lightly pluck stray hair from the insides of the ears.
- Cut the tips of the toenails with the toenail clipper, being careful not to cut the quick.
- Clean the eyes by wiping with damp cotton. If the eyes are excessively watery and sticky, snip the stained hair from the corners with scissors.
- Using the #10 blade, shave the anal area, being certain not to put the blade in direct contact with the skin.
- Using the #10 blade, shave the abdomen from groin to navel and down the insides of the thighs.

128

- Putting a cotton ball in each ear prevents water from entering the ear canals. Once this is done, bathe the dog and fluff dry him.
- Using the medium metal comb, part the coat down the center of the back from the top of the head to the base of the tail. Next, part the hair from the top of the head to the tip of the nose.
- Comb through the entire coat, first with the medium and then the fine metal comb.
- Comb the tail thoroughly.
- Scissor the hair between the pads of the feet. Comb the hair on the legs downward, and while the dog is standing, scissor around the edges of the feet to give a round effect.
- Some owners prefer the topknot tied in a ponytail fashion. To do this, part the hair on the head from the corner of each eye to the front corner of each ear and across the head from ear to ear. Gather this hair, comb through evenly and slightly to the back, and secure it with a rubber band. An alternative is to make a braid and secure the end with a rubber band. Attach a bow to either of the rubber bands.
- Comb the entire coat and tail with a fine metal comb.

Some dog owners use cream rinse and similar products on these dogs, but I have found, through experience, that these products cause the coats to become more matted in the long run. A good protein-enriched shampoo is entirely adequate. The long-coated Lhasa Apso should be groomed every 2 or 3 weeks. The ears should be checked weekly (cleaned if necessary) and the nails should be checked at the grooming sessions.. For owners who prefer a short, cuddly look, use the Teddy Bear Clip. See General Information section. For owners who like the long-haired look, even during the heat of the summer, the entire undercoat can be thinned out so that the dog will be more comfortable. The same instructions apply for grooming, bathing, and fluff drying the Lhasa Apso (*i.e.,* steps 1-7). Part the coat, using the medium metal comb, about 1½" to 2" from the center of the back, down one side. Comb the top hair to the other side (so you do not touch the outer coat), and with thinning shears, thin out the remaining undercoat about 1" at a time. Repeat on the opposite side and across the chest and thighs. Part the coat down the center of the back and thoroughly comb through it, first with the medium and then with the fine metal comb. Tie the topknot and scissor the feet, as mentioned before in the grooming instructions for Lhasa Apsos.

MALTESE

Tools and Equipment

Slicker brush. Matting comb. Metal combs (medium/fine). Medicated ear powder. Nail clipper. Eye drops (eye stain remover). Oster A-5 clipper. #10 blade. Rubber bands. Cotton balls. Scissors.

Grooming Procedure

- Starting with the head, brush the entire coat and tail with the slicker brush, removing any mats with the matting comb. Comb through the coat, using the medium-toothed metal comb.
- Clean the ears, using the medicated ear powder, and lightly pluck stray hair from the inside of the ears.
- Cut the tips of the toenails with the toenail clipper, being careful not to cut the quick.
- Clean the eyes by wiping with cotton that has been moistened with eye drops. If the eyes are excessively watery and sticky, with scissors snip the stained hair from the corners.
- Using a #10 blade, shave the anal area, being certain not to put the blade in direct contact with the skin (½″ on either side).

130

- Using the #10 blade, shave the abdomen from groin to navel and down the insides of the thighs.
- Place a cotton ball in each ear (this prevents water from entering the ear canals) and bathe the dog. Fluff dry him.
- Using the medium metal comb, part the coat down the center of the back, from the top of the head to the base of the tail. Then part the hair from the top of the head to the tip of the nose. Comb all hair downward from the part. An alternative is to make a part on the head from the outer corner of each eye to the front corner of each ear and across the head from ear to ear. Comb this hair evenly, slightly to the back, and secure it with a rubber band. Attach a bow.
- Scissor the hair between the pads of the feet. Comb the hair on the legs downward, and while the dog is standing, scissor the edges of the feet to give a round effect.
- Comb the entire coat downward with the fine metal comb.

Some dog groomers use cream rinse and similar products on these dogs, but I have found, through experience, that these products cause the coat to become more matted in the long run. A good protein-enriched shampoo is entirely adequate.. The long-haired Maltese should be groomed every 4 weeks. The owner should brush and comb the dog on a regular basis, thus preventing the coat from becoming matted. The ears should be checked weekly (cleaned if necessary) and the nails should be checked at the grooming session.. For Maltese owners who prefer a short, easy to keep, cuddly look, refer to the Teddy Bear Clip in the General Information section.

Miniature Schnauzer

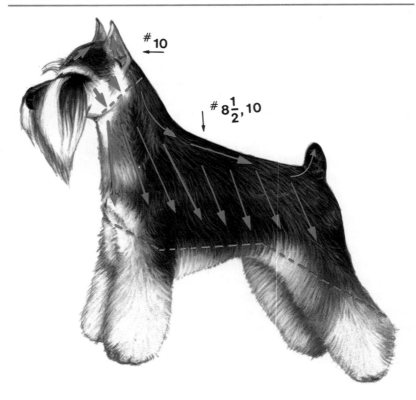

#10

$$\#8\tfrac{1}{2}, 10$$

Tools and Equipment

Electric clipper. #10, #15, #8½ blades. Scissors, regular straight edge. Scissors, small blunt tip. Metal comb. Pin brush. Nail clipper. Liquid ear cleaner.

Grooming Procedure

- Begin with a rough clip outline *before* bathing. Start with the body, using either an #8½ or #10 blade. Run the clipper from occiput (top of skull) down the sides of the neck. Clip down the body to the elbow, on the shoulders, and on the chest. Always follow the lay of the hair. Continue clipping down the sides of the body to the underbelly. Leave "fringe" for later scissoring.
- Finish clipping the body, tail, and rear legs in an even pattern with the same blade. Stay about 2″ above the rear hocks. Leave leg furnishings on the stifle. Clip around and under the tail. Move the blade downward to clean the vent area. Use caution and a light touch so as not to cause clipper burn. Never leave an "apron" on the chest or rear.

132

- Clip the head from the top of the eyebrows to the top of the skull. Clip the cheeks and throat with the body blade. Clip the ears inside and out with a #15 blade. Again, use caution to avoid clipper burn on these sensitive areas.
- Lift the dog by his front legs. With a #15 blade, clean the belly to the navel, the hindquarters, and one-third the way down the inner thighs. Leave outer fringe on the belly edge and on the stifle.
- Bathe the dog. Towel dry him by squeezing water out of the legs and beard. Comb through the legs and beard while wet, using a detangler solution if necessary. Cut toenails *now* while they are soft from bathing.
- Fluff dry, using a pin brush up and out on the legs. Pin brush down on the eyebrows and beard. Drying can be completed in a cage.

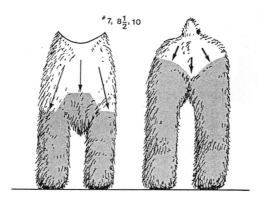

- The Miniature Schnauzer is now ready for scissoring. Start with the head. Comb the eyebrows and beard down and forward. Scissor the brows by slanting your scissor points toward the base of the ear. Scissor between the brows in a diamond shape. Clean out hair from the inner ear with blunt scissors, a hemostat, and liquid ear cleaner. Scissor off the edges of the ears. The Miniature Schnauzer head should appear rectangular, never round. Scissor the lower chest, between the legs, as flat and smooth as possible.
- Fluff and comb up the hair on the legs. Scissor the elbows close to the body. Scissor down the front legs to achieve a barber pole effect. The rear legs are scissored to give an arc-like shape to the stifle, and the hocks are scissored evenly. Scissor around the toes and under the foot pads. *Never cut hair from between the toes.* Strive for straight legs.
- Underbelly fringe should be scissored to the shape of the body, never leaving more than 1 or 2 inches in depth.

133

Newfoundland

Tools and Equipment

Slicker brush. Steel comb (fine/medium). Protein coat conditioner. High velocity dryer. Long hair molting comb (#565). Scissor. Pin brush. Nail clipper (extra large). Ear cleaner. Medicated ear powder. #10 blade. Tearless protein shampoo. Oster A-5 clipper. Cotton balls. Thinning shear.

Grooming Procedure

- Spray the entire coat with protein coat conditioner. This adds body to the coat and helps repair split ends. Brush through the entire coat with the pin brush. This will loosen up the coat and remove dead undercoat. Start at the rear of the dog, at the bottom of the skirt area. Work in sections, using your other hand to lift the hair ahead of the section you are working on. Work through the entire dog from the back to the neck area. Then brush through the coat with the slicker brush to remove the top dead coat. Work vigorously. The more hair you remove now, the less hair you need to wash and dry.
- Swab the ears with a cotton ball that has been moistened with ear cleaner. This will remove the dirt and control ear odor. Follow this with a dry cotton ball and dust the ears with medicated ear powder.
- Cut the nails with a guillotine-type nail trimmer. Nails should be cut monthly.

134

- Bathe the dog with a tearless protein shampoo that is pH-alkaline. This adds body to the coat and restructures damaged hair.
- Use a high velocity dryer to blow excess water off the dog while the dog is still in the tub. This will speed up the drying time and help prevent the coat from becoming overly dry. Cage dry the dog until the hair is damp. Then finish drying him on the table, using a blow dryer and a pin brush to separate all the hair and remove all of the loose coat. Finish with a steel comb through the entire coat, paying special attention to the fine hair behind the ears. Use the fine side of the comb for this area.
- Scissor any long hair under the tail that hangs over the anus. Be sure the anus is clear, and then use the #10 blade to blend down under the tail area so it does not collect fecal matter.
- Check between the foot pads and under the feet for burrs, tar, etc. Scissor the hair under the feet even with the pads. Trim any hair around the paw that touches the ground and neaten the entire foot. With thinning shears, trim the hair growing between the toes.
- The whiskers may be removed with a scissor to improve expression; however, this is optional.
- Lightly mist the coat with protein coat conditioner to add brilliance and fragrance.

NORWEGIAN ELKHOUND

Tools and Equipment

Slicker brush. Undercoat rake. Pure boar bristle brush. Comb (fine/medium). Tearless protein shampoo. Scissor. Pin brush. Thinning shear. Ear cleaner. Medicated ear powder. Protein coat conditioner. High velocity dryer. Nail clipper. Cotton balls.

Grooming Procedure

- Spray the entire coat with protein coat conditioner. This adds body to the coat and helps repair split ends. Brush through the entire coat with the undercoat rake. This will loosen up the coat and remove dead undercoat. Start at the rear of the dog, at the bottom of the skirt area. Work in sections, using your other hand to lift the hair ahead of the section you are working on. Work through the entire dog from the back to the neck area. Then brush through the coat with a slicker brush to remove the top dead coat. Work vigorously. The more hair you remove now, the less hair you need to wash and dry.

- Swab the ears with a cotton ball that has been moistened with ear cleaner. This will remove dirt and control ear odor. Follow with a dry cotton ball and dust the ears with medicated ear powder.
- Cut the nails with a guillotine-type nail trimmer. Nails should be cut monthly.
- Check between the foot pads and under the feet for burrs, tar, etc. Scissor the hair under the feet to prevent debris from adhering. With a thinning shear, trim any hair around the paw that touches the ground or grows out between the paws.
- Bathe the dog with a tearless protein shampoo that is pH-alkaline. This will add fullness and body to the coat and restructure damaged hair.
- Use a high velocity dryer to blow excess water off the dog while the dog is still in the tub. This will speed up the drying time and help prevent the coat from becoming overly dry. Cage dry the dog until the hair is damp. Then finish drying on the table, using a blow dryer and a pin brush to separate all the hair and remove all of the loose coat.
- Brush the entire coat, using the dryer to style and separate the hair. Be sure to brush to the skin. Follow by combing the entire coat with the medium-toothed comb. Use the *fine* part of the comb on the soft hair behind the ears.
- The whiskers may be removed with scissors to improve expression.
- Spray your pure bristle brush with protein coat conditioner and top brush the coat to add brilliance and fragrance.

OLD ENGLISH SHEEPDOG

Tools and Equipment
Slicker brush. Mat-splitting comb. Metal comb (medium). Toenail clipper. Eye drops (eye stain remover). Cotton balls. Scissors. Thinning shears. Oster A-5 clipper. #10 blade.

Grooming Procedure
- Starting at the head, thoroughly brush the entire coat with the slicker brush. Remove any mats with the mat-splitting comb. Comb through the coat to remove all loosened hair. If the dog is excessively matted, start at the feet and brush the legs upward in sections. On the body work from rear to front in the same manner.
- Clean the ears, using the medicated ear powder, and lightly pluck any stray hair from the insides.
- Clean the eyes by wiping with cotton that has been moistened with eye drops. This will also help to remove stains under or around the eyes.

- Cut the tips of the toenails with the nail clipper, being careful not to cut to the quick.
- With the #10 blade, shave the anal area, being certain not to put the blade in direct contact with the skin (½" each side).
- Shave the abdomen from groin to navel and down the insides of the thighs.
- Putting a cotton ball in each ear prevents water from entering the ear canals. Now you're ready to bathe the dog. Cage dry him, so as to remove excess water.
- Lift the dog onto a grooming table and complete the drying with a blow dryer and slicker brush.
- Scissor the hair between the pads of the feet; while the dog is standing, lightly scissor around the edges of the feet to make a neat appearance.
- Using the thinning shears on the rump, make it appear nice and round. The rump should slope into the rear end.
- Brush the body hair to make it full and fluffy and brush the leg hair downward.

The Old English Sheepdog should be groomed every 3 or 4 weeks, although regular brushing by the owner will help maintain a healthy coat and keep it free of tangles. The ears should be checked weekly and cleaned if necessary, and the toenails should be checked and cut at the grooming session.

PEKINGESE

Tools and Equipment

Slicker brush. Matting comb (medium). Medicated ear powder. Nail clipper. Eye drops (eye stain remover). Medicated talcum powder. #10 blade. Cotton balls. Scissors.

Grooming Procedure

- Brush the entire coat and tail with the slicker brush, starting at the head and working down the back. Remove any mats with the matting comb. When brushing the legs, start at the feet and work up. Comb through the coat with the metal comb.
- Clean the ears, using the medicated ear powder, and lightly pluck any stray hair from the insides of the ears.
- Cut the tips of the toenails with the toenail clipper, being careful not to cut the quick.

- Clean the eyes by wiping with cotton that has been moistened with eye drops. If the eyes are excessively watery and sticky, with scissors, snip stained hair from the corners.
- Clean the furrows on the face with moistened cotton. Daily use of eye drops or medicated talcum powder on the furrows will keep them dry and help prevent soreness or infection.
- Using the #10 blade, shave the anal area, being certain not to put the blade in direct contact with the skin (½" on either side).
- Using the #10 blade, shave the abdomen from groin to navel and down the insides of the thighs.
- Place a cotton ball in each ear (this prevents water from entering the ear canals) and bathe the dog. Towel dry him.
- Place the dog on the grooming table and fluff dry with the slicker brush, brushing the coat in an upward motion for a fuller, thicker look.
- With scissors, snip the hair between the pads of the feet and the toes. Snip around the edges of the feet for a neat effect.
- Comb through the tail, using the metal comb. Make a part down the center and allow it to fall naturally across the dog's back.

The Pekingese should be groomed every 6 or 8 weeks, depending on the fullness of the coat. The owner should brush the dog on a regular basis. This breed is prone to skin inflammation and "hot spots," especially around the area where the tail falls on his back and also during the shedding season. The itching and irritation can be relieved by the groomer's or owner's applying a Sulfadene-moistened cotton ball to the affected area or by bathing the dog in Sulfadene shampoo every two weeks. The dog's owner should check with a veterinarian before using any medicated products.

Pembroke Welsh Corgi

Tools and Equipment

Slicker brush (gentle). Steel comb (medium/fine). Pure boar bristle brush. Short hair molting comb (#564). Scissors. Eye stain remover. Ear cleaner. Medicated ear powder. Protein coat conditioner. Tearless protein shampoo. Cotton balls. Nail clipper.

Grooming Procedure

- Spray the entire coat with protein coat conditioner. This adds body to the coat and helps repair split ends. Brush through the entire coat with the gentle slicker to remove loose hair. Then comb with the molting comb made for short-haired breeds (#564) to take out loose undercoat.
- Swab the ears with a cotton ball that has been moistened with ear cleaner. This will remove dirt and control ear odor. Follow this with a dry cotton ball and dust the ears with medicated ear powder.
- Cut the nails with a guillotine-type nail trimmer. Nails should be cut monthly.
- Bathe the dog with a tearless protein shampoo that is pH-alkaline. This will add fullness and body to the coat and restructure damaged hair.

140

- Cage dry the dog until damp. Finish drying on the table, using a blow dryer and a pure bristle brush. Thoroughly comb through the entire dog.
- Check between the foot pads and under the feet for burrs, tar, etc. Scissor the hair under the feet even with the pads. Trim any hair around the paw that touches the ground and neaten the entire foot. Use thinning shears to trim the hair growing between the toes. Be sure to neaten the hair on the back of the rear pasterns.
- The whiskers may be removed with scissors to improve the expression (optional).
- Top brush with a pure bristle brush that has been sprayed with protein coat conditioner. This adds brilliance and fragrance to the coat.

POINTER

Tools and Equipment

Sisal (natural bristle) brush). Toenail clipper. Lanolin coat conditioner. Eye drops (eye stain remover). Chamois cloth. Cotton balls. Scissors.

141

Grooming Procedure

- Brush the coat briskly with the sisal brush.
- Clean the ears using the medicated ear powder.
- Clean the eyes by wiping with cotton that has been moistened with eye drops. This will also help in removing any stains.
- Cut the tips of the nails with the toenail clipper, being careful not to cut the quick.
- Using scissors, clip the whiskers from the muzzle, from the chin, from the sides of the face, and from above the eyes. (Note: Clipping the whiskers is a decision to be left to the owner if the dog is not a show dog.)
- Putting a cotton ball in each ear prevents water from entering the ear canals. Bathe and then cage dry the dog.
- Put a few drops of lanolin coat conditioner into the palms of your hands, rub together lightly, and gently massage this into the coat.
- Brush the coat with the sisal brush to distribute the conditioner; then lightly rub over the coat with the chamois cloth to give it a nice sheen.

The Pointer should be bathed every 8 or 10 weeks. Regular brushing by the owner between baths helps maintain a healthy, shiny coat. The ears should be checked weekly and cleaned if necessary, and the toenails should be checked monthly and cut if necessary.

POMERANIAN

Tools and Equipment

Nail clipper (guillotine or scissor). Styptic powder. Ear cleaner. Cotton balls. Shampoo (conditioning or all-purpose). Slicker brush. Comb. Straight scissors.

Grooming Procedure

- Nails should be cut by removing the tips only. Avoid cutting the

quick; however, if the nail should bleed, apply styptic powder to stop the bleeding. Any rough nail edges may be smoothed with a file.

- Clean the ears with a liquid cleaner by applying the liquid to a cotton ball and wiping all accumulated wax and dirt from the crevices in both ears.
- Brush through the entire dog to remove mats and dead hair.
- Bathe the dog in your shampoo of choice. Rinse thoroughly. A cream rinse may be used to help remove dead hair and cut down on static electricity.
- Towel dry the dog until he is just damp. A blow dryer will have to be used to finish drying him. While blowing the coat dry, brush through the coat. The hair may be brushed *against* the growth to give an added fullness to the coat.
- With scissors, remove excess hair between the foot pads and on the bottom of the feet. The hair that grows between the toes on the top of the foot may be removed to tighten up the foot. Excess hair on the back of the hock may be removed, as well as stray hairs in the ears.
- The hair around the anal area should be trimmed close.
- Comb through the entire dog to make sure all knots and tangles have been removed.

The completed Pomeranian should resemble a "powder puff," and it should be groomed every 6 to 8 weeks.

Poodle, Kennel clip

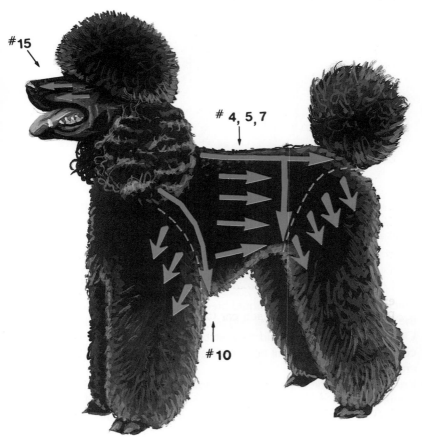

#15

4, 5, 7

#10

Tools and Equipment
 Slicker brush. Mat-splitting comb. Metal rake. Metal combs
 (medium/wide). Toenail clipper. Eye drops (eye stain remover).
 Medicated ear powder. Oster A-5 clipper. #15, #10, #7, #5, #4
 blades. Cotton balls. Scissors.

Grooming Procedure
 ●Brush the coat thoroughly with the slicker brush, using upward
 strokes. Remove any mats or tangles with the mat-splitting comb
 and/or metal rake. Comb through the coat with the medium comb,
 removing all loosened hair.
 ●Clean the ears, using the medicated ear powder, and lightly pluck
 any stray hair from the insides.
 ●Clean the eyes by wiping with cotton that has been moistened with
 eye drops. This will also help to remove any stains.
 144

- Cut the tips of the toenails with the nail clipper, being careful not to cut the quick.
- With the #15 blade, shave the feet. Start by shaving between the pads, then shave up just clear of the largest pad. This becomes the shave line for the whole foot. Make sure there are no hairs left on or between the toes.
- Shave the face, selecting a style from Poodle Heads and Faces.
- Shave the tail one-third of the length from the base.
- With the #10 blade, shave the abdomen from groin to navel and down the insides of the thighs.
- Shave the anal area (#10 blade), being certain not to put the blade in direct contact with the skin (½" each side).
- With the #7, #5, or #4 blade (depending on the length of coat desired), clip down the back from the base of the skull to the base of the tail.
- From the base of the ears, clip down the shoulders to the tops of the front legs.
- Clip down the front and between the front legs.
- From the first clip down the back, clip down the sides of the abdomen and underneath it.
- Clip down the hips to the tops of the rear legs.
- Comb through the coat with the wide-toothed comb to remove excess hair.
- Place a cotton ball in each ear (this prevents water from entering the ear canals) and bathe the dog. Fluff dry, using the slicker brush in an upward motion.
- Brush the clipped area on the body and comb the legs upward with the wide-toothed comb.
- Using the same blade as before, repeat the process for the pattern, blending the hair into the tops of the legs.
- Comb the hair on the front legs by the ankles downward and scissor straight around.
- With the wide-toothed comb, fluff up the hair on the front legs and scissor it into short, straight tubular shapes that taper at the tops and blend into the body.
- Comb downward the hair on the rear legs by the ankles and scissor straight around.
- With the wide-toothed comb, fluff up the hair on the rear legs and scissor them short, following the natural contours and blending into the hips.
- Fluff up the hair on the legs and trim any straggly hairs, especially around the ankles.
- Scissor the tail into a full, round pom-pom.
- Comb the hair on the head straight up and scissor around the edges. Fluff up the hair with the wide-toothed comb and scissor it round on top, tapering it into the ears and the neck.

Poodle, Dutch clip

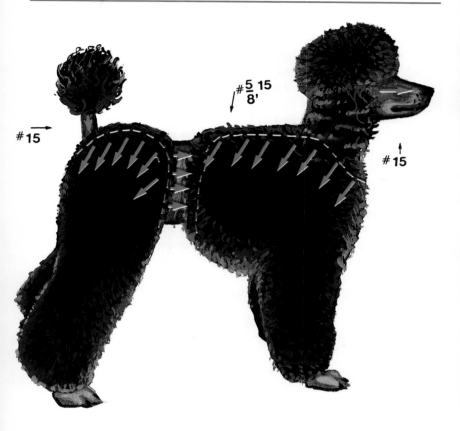

#15

#$\frac{5}{8}$' 15

#15

Tools and Equipment

Slicker brush. Mat-splitting comb. Metal rake. Metal combs (medium/wide). Toenail clipper. Eye drops (eye stain remover). Medicated ear powder. Oster A-5 clipper. #15, #10, #⅞, #⅝, #7 blades. Cotton balls. Scissors.

Grooming Procedure

- Brush the coat thoroughly with the slicker brush, using upward strokes. Remove any mats or tangles with the mat-splitting comb and/or metal rake. Comb through the coat with the medium comb, removing all loosened hair.
- Clean the ears, using the medicated ear powder, and lightly pluck any stray hair from the insides.
- Clean the eyes by wiping with cotton that has been moistened with eye drops. This will also help to remove any stains under or around the eyes.

146

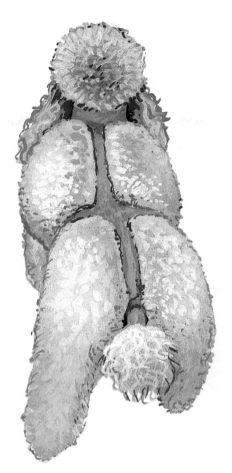

- Cut the tips of the nails with the toenail clipper, being careful not to cut the quick.
- With the #15 blade, shave the feet. Start by shaving between the pads, and then shave up just clear of the largest pad—this will be the shave line for the whole foot. Make sure there are no hairs left on or between the toes.
- Shave the face, selecting a style from Poodle Heads and Faces.
- Shave the tail one-third of the length from the base.
- With the #10 blade, shave the abdomen from groin to navel and down the insides of the thighs.
- Shave the anal area with a #10 blade, being certain not to put the blade in direct contact with the skin (½" each side).
- With the #15 blade, shave around the neck one blade width from the base of the ears, base of the skull, and under the jaw. This pattern line should reach a point at just above the shoulder on a small dog. (Increase the blade width with the size of the dog, so that the pattern line reaches that point.)
- With the #⅝ blade (for toys), #⅞ blade (for miniatures), or #15

blade (for standards), shave the pattern line straight down the center of the back, from the neck pattern to the base of the tail.

- Using the same blade, shave from the center back pattern down the sides at the flanks (this line should be just in front of the rear legs).
- Comb through the coat with the medium comb to remove excess hair.
- Place a cotton ball in each ear (this prevents water from entering the ear canals) and bathe the dog. Fluff dry, using the slicker brush in an upward motion.
- Brush through the coat and fluff up, with the wide-toothed comb, all areas to be scissored.
- Using the same blades as before, repeat the process for the pattern, this time shaving *against* the lay of the coat for a clean sharp look.
- With the #15 blade, shaving against the lay of the coat, round off all pattern corners.
- With the #7 blade on the Oster clipper, lightly blend the hair down from the pattern. Scissor all straggly hairs from the edges.
- With the wide-toothed comb, fluff up the hair on the body and scissor evenly into a full, round barrel shape.
- Scissor the chest, between the front legs and underneath, even with the body.
- Comb downward the hair on the front legs by the ankles and scissor straight around.
- With the wide-toothed comb, fluff up the hair on the front legs and scissor into straight tubular shapes, blending into the body.
- Comb the hair on the rear legs by the ankles downward and scissor straight around.
- With the wide-toothed comb, fluff up the hair on the rear legs and scissor into straight, full shapes to make them appear roundish on the hips.
- Scissor the tail into a full, round pom-pom.
- Comb the hair on the head straight up and scissor around the edges. Fluff up the hair with the wide-toothed comb and scissor it round on top, tapering it into the ears and neck.
- With the comb, fluff up the hair on the legs and body; trim any straggly hairs, especially around the ankles, with the scissors.

The Poodle should be groomed every 4 to 6 weeks, depending on the thickness of the coat and how fast it grows. Regular brushing and combing by the owner, between groomings, will help keep the coat healthy and free of tangles. The ears should be checked weekly and cleaned if necessary, and the toenails should be checked and cut at the grooming session. It should be noted that all shaved areas should be shaved *against* the lay of the coat, except on a dog with sensitive skin. In this case use a #10 blade and shave *with* the lay of the coat. The pattern should be shaved with the lay of the coat prior to the bath and against the lay of the coat afterward.

Poodle, Lamb clip

#4,5,7

#15

Tools and Equipment

Slicker brush. Mat-splitting comb. Metal rake. Metal combs (medium/wide). Toenail clipper. Eye drops (eye stain remover). Medicated ear powder. Oster A-5 clipper. #15, #10, #7, #5, #4 blades. Cotton balls. Scissors.

Grooming Procedure

- Brush the coat thoroughly with the slicker brush, using upward strokes. Remove any mats or tangles with the mat-splitting comb and/or metal rake. Comb through the coat with the medium comb, removing all loosened hair.
- Clean the ears, using the medicated ear powder, and lightly pluck any stray hair from the insides.
- Clean the eyes by wiping with cotton that has been moistened with eye drops. This helps to remove any stains around the eyes.
- Cut the tips of the toenails with the nail clipper, being careful not to cut the quick.
- With the #15 blade, shave the feet. Start by shaving between the pads, then shave up just clear of the largest pad. This becomes the shave line for the whole foot. Make sure there are no hairs left on or between the toes.

- Shave the face. Select a style from Poodle Heads and Faces.
- Shave the tail one-third of the length from the base.
- With the #10 blade, shave the abdomen from groin to navel and down the insides of the thighs.
- Shave the anal area (#10 blade), being certain not to put the blade in direct contact with the skin (½" each side).
- With the #7, #5, or #4 blade (depending on the length of coat desired), clip down the back from the base of the skull to the base of the tail.
- From the base of the ears, clip down to the shoulders and down the front to the breastbone.
- From the first clip down the back, clip down the sides of the abdomen and over the hips.
- Comb through the coat with the medium comb to remove excess hair.
- Put a cotton ball in each ear (this prevents water from entering the ear canals) and bathe the dog. Fluff dry, using the slicker brush in an upward motion.
- Brush up the clipped area on the body and fluff up the legs with the wide-toothed comb.
- Using the same blades as before, repeat the process for the pattern, blending the hair into the chest, lower stomach, and tops of the legs.
- Scissor evenly the chest, between the front legs and under the abdomen, and blend this area into the body. (Note: It is acceptable to use the same body blade on these areas.)
- Comb the hair on the front legs by the ankles downward and scissor straight around.
- With the wide-toothed comb, fluff up the hair on the front legs and scissor into straight tubular shapes, tapering them slightly at the tops and blending into the body and shoulders.
- Comb downward the hair on the rear legs by the ankles and scissor straight around.
- With the wide-toothed comb, fluff up the hair on the rear legs and scissor it into straight full shapes, blending into the body at the hips.
- Scissor the tail into a full round pom-pom.
- Comb the hair on the head straight up and scissor around the edges. Fluff up the hair with the wide-toothed comb and scissor it round on top, tapering it into the ears and neck.
- With the comb, fluff up all the hair on the legs and trim any straggly hairs, especially around the ankles, with the scissors.

The Poodle should be groomed every 4 to 6 weeks, depending on the thickness of the coat and how fast it grows. Regular brushing and combing by the owner, between groomings, will help keep the coat healthy and free of tangles. The ears should be checked weekly and cleaned if necessary, and the toenails should be checked and cut.

POODLE, PUPPY CLIP

#10 →

#10 ←

#8½ ↑

#15 →

Tools and Equipment

Slicker brush. Mat-splitting comb. Metal rake. Metal combs (medium/wide). Toenail clipper. Eye drops (eye stain remover). Medicated ear powder. Oster A-5 clipper. #15, #10, #8½ blades. Cotton balls. Scissors.

Grooming Procedure

- Brush the coat thoroughly with upward strokes, using the slicker brush. Remove any mats or tangles with the mat-splitting comb and/or metal rake. Comb through the coat with the medium comb, removing all excess hair.
- Clean the ears, using the medicated ear powder, and lightly pluck any stray hair from the insides.
- Clean the eyes by wiping with cotton that has been moistened with eye drops. This will also help in removing any stains around the eyes.

151

- Cut the tips of the toenails with the nail clipper, being careful not to cut the quick.
- With the #15 blade, shave the feet. Start by shaving between the pads, then shave up just clear of the largest pad. This becomes the shave line for the whole foot. Make sure there are no hairs left on or between the toes.
- With the #10 blade, shave the face. Select a style from Poodle Heads and Faces.
- With the #10 blade, shave the tail one-third of the length from the base.
- With the #8½ blade, shave the abdomen from groin to navel and down the insides of the thighs.
- Shave the anal area (#8½ blade), being certain not to put the blade in direct contact with the skin (½" each side).
- Comb through the coat with the wide-toothed comb to remove excess hair.
- Place a cotton ball in each ear (this prevents water from entering the ear canals) and bathe the dog. Fluff dry, using the slicker brush in an upward motion.
- Brush the entire coat upward and fluff it up with the wide-toothed comb.
- Scissor the entire body to an even length (1" to 2" or whatever length is desired by the owner).
- Comb the hair on the front legs by the ankles downward and scissor straight around.
- Fluff up the hair on the front legs with the wide-toothed comb and scissor into straight tubular shapes, blending them into the body.
- Comb downward the hair on the rear legs by the ankles and scissor straight around.
- With the wide-toothed comb, fluff up the hair on the rear legs and scissor them straight and full. Blend these areas into the body.
- Scissor the tail into a full, round pom-pom.
- Comb back the hair on the head and scissor around the front edge, across the eyes to the ears. Fluff up the remaining hair with the comb, and scissor it round on the top. Blend this into the body, around the neck, and into the ears.
- With the comb, fluff up all hair and trim any straggly hairs with the scissors, especially around the ankles.

The Poodle should be groomed every 4 to 6 weeks, depending on the thickness of the coat and how fast it grows. Regular brushing and combing by the owner, between groomings, will help keep the coat healthy and free of tangles. By the time the puppy reaches 6 to 8 months, the owner may consider one of the other Poodle clips. The ears should be checked weekly and cleaned if necessary, and the toenails should be checked and cut at the grooming session. It should be noted that a Poodle puppy's skin is usually sensitive, so use the #10 blade on the face and tail, shaving *with* the lay of the coat.

POODLE, ROYAL DUTCH

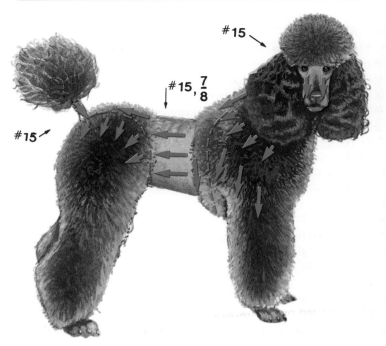

#15

#15, $\frac{7}{8}$

#15

Tools and Equipment

Slicker brush. Mat-splitting comb. metal rake. metal combs (medium/wide). Toenail clipper. Eye drops (eye stain remover). Medicated ear powder. Oster A-5 clipper. #15, #10, #7, #⅞ blades. Cotton balls. Scissors.

Grooming Procedure

- Brush the coat thoroughly with the slicker brush, using upward strokes. Remove any mats or tangles with the mat-splitting comb and/or metal rake. Comb through the coat with the medium comb, removing all loosened hair.
- Clean the ears, using the medicated ear powder, and lightly pluck any stray hair from the insides.
- Clean the eyes by wiping with cotton that has been moistened with eye drops. This will also help in removing any stains around the eyes.
- Cut the tips of the toenails ,being careful not to cut the quick.
- With the #15 blade, shave the feet. Start by shaving between the pads, then shave up just clear of the largest pad. This becomes the shave line for the whole foot. Make sure there are no hairs left on or between the toes.
- Shave the face, selecting a style from Poodle Heads and Faces.
- Shave the tail one-third of the length from the base.

153

- With the #10 blade, shave the abdomen from groin to navel and down the insides of the thighs.
- Shave the anal area (#10 blade), being certain not to put the blade in direct contact with the skin (½″ each side).
- With the #15 blade, shave around the neck, one blade-width from the base of the ears, base of the skull, and under the jaw. This pattern line should reach to a point just above the shoulder on a small dog. (Increase the blade width with the size of the dog, so that the pattern line reaches that point).
- With the #⅞ blade (for toys/small miniatures) or #15 blade (for miniatures/standards), shave a pattern line straight down the center of the back, from the neck pattern to the base of the tail.
- Using the same blade, shave from the center back pattern down the sides at the flanks. (This line should fall just in front of the rear legs).
- Comb through the coat with the medium comb to remove excess hair.
- Place a cotton ball in each ear (this prevents water from entering the ear canal) and bathe the dog. Fluff dry, using the slicker brush in an upward motion.
- Brush through the coat, and fluff up with the wide-toothed comb, all areas to be scissored.
- Using the same blades as before, repeat the process for the pattern, this time shaving *against* the lay of the coat for a clean sharp look.
- With the #15 blade, and shaving *against* the lay of the coat, round off all pattern corners.
- With the #7 blade, lightly blend the hair down from the pattern. Scissor all straggly hairs from the edges.
- With the wide-toothed comb, fluff up the hair on the body and scissor it evenly into a full, round barrel shape.
- Scissor the chest, between the front legs and underneath, even with the body.
- Comb downward the hair on the front legs by the ankle and scissor straight around.
- With the wide-toothed comb, fluff up the hair on the front legs and scissor it into straight, tubular shapes. Blend these areas into the body.
- Comb the hair on the rear legs by the ankles downward and scissor straight around.
- With the wide-toothed comb, fluff up the hair on the rear legs and scissor it into straight, full shapes that appear roundish on the hips.
- Scissor the tail into a full, round pom-pom.
- Comb the hair on the head straight up and scissor around the edges. Fluff up the hair with the wide-toothed comb and scissor it round on top, tapering it into the ears and neck.
- With the comb, fluff up all the hair on the legs and body and trim any straggly hairs, especially around the ankles, with the scissors.

POODLE, SUMMER CLIP

#10, 15

#7, 10

#15

Tools and Equipment
Slicker brush. Mat-splitting comb. Metal rake. Metal combs (medium/wide). Toenail clipper. Eye drops (eye stain remover). Medicated ear powder. Oster A-5 clipper. #15, #10, #7 blades. Cotton balls. Scissors.

Grooming Procedure
- Brush the coat thoroughly with upward strokes, using the slicker brush. Remove any mats or tangles with the mat-splitting comb and/or metal rake. Comb through the coat with the medium comb, removing all loosened hair.
- Clean the ears, using the medicated ear powder, and lightly pluck any stray hair from the insides.
- Clean the eyes by wiping with cotton that has been moistened with eye drops. This will also help remove any stains around the eyes.
- Cut the tips of the toenails with the nail clipper, being careful not to cut the quick.
- With the #15 blade, shave the feet. Start by shaving between the pads, then shave up just clear of the largest pad. This becomes the shave line for the whole foot. Make sure there are no hairs left on or between the toes.
- Shave the face, selecting a style from Poodle Heads and Faces.
- Shave the tail one-third of the length from the base.

- With the #10 blade, shave the abdomen from groin to navel and down the insides of the thighs.
- Shave the anal area (#10 blade), being certain not to put the blade in direct contact with the skin (½" each side).
- With the #10 or #7 blade, clip the entire body from the base of the skull (neck area) to the base of the tail; down the chest; between the front legs; and around and under the stomach.
- Continue clipping down the legs to a point just above the elbows on the front legs and to the hock joints on the rear legs.
- To remove excess hair, comb through the remaining hair on the head, ears, tail, and ankles.
- Place a cotton ball in each ear (this prevents water from entering the ear canals) and bathe the dog. Fluff dry, using the slicker brush in an upward motion.
- Lightly brush up the clipped area on the body and legs, and using the same blade as before, repeat the process for the pattern.
- With the wide-toothed comb, fluff up the hair on the head, ankles, and tail.
- Comb downward the hair on the ankles and scissor it straight around; then comb this hair upward and again scissor straight around. Now fluff the hair out with the comb and scissor into round pom-poms.
- Scissor the tail into a full, round pom-pom.
- Comb the hair on the head straight up and scissor around the edges. Fluff up the hair with the wide-toothed comb and scissor it round on top, tapering into the ears and neck.

The Poodle should be groomed every 4 to 6 weeks, depending on the thickness of the coat and how fast it grows. Regular brushing and combing by the owner, between groomings, will help keep the coat healthy and free of tangles. The ears should be checked weekly and cleaned if necessary, and the toenails should be checked and cut at the grooming session. It should be noted that all shaved areas should be shaved *against* the lay of the coat, except on a dog with sensitive skin. Then use a #10 blade and shave *with* the lay of the coat. In this clip, also known as the Clown clip, the body and legs are also shaved with the lay of the coat.

POODLE, TOWN AND COUNTRY CLIP

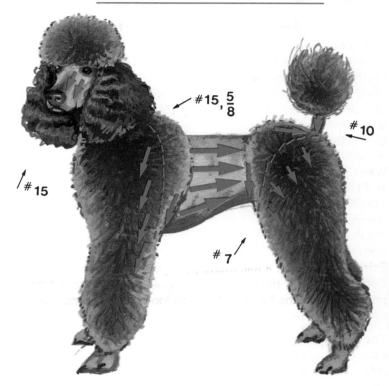

#15, $\frac{5}{8}$

#10

#15

#7

Tools and Equipment

Slicker brush. Mat-splitting comb. Metal rake. Metal combs (medium/wide). Toenail clipper. Eye drops (eye stain remover). Medicated ear powder. Oster A-5 clipper. #15, #10, #7, #⅝ blades. Cotton balls. Scissors.

Grooming Procedure

- Brush the coat thoroughly with the slicker brush, using upward strokes. Remove any mats or tangles with the mat-splitting comb and/or metal rake. Comb through the coat with the medium comb, removing all loosened hair.
- Clean the ears, using the medicated ear powder, and lightly pluck any stray hair from the insides.
- Clean the eyes by wiping with cotton that has been moistened with eye drops. This will also help to remove any stains under or around the eyes.
- Cut the tips of the toenails with the nail clipper, being careful not to cut the quick.

157

- With the #15 blade, shave the feet. Start by shaving between the pads, then shave up just clear of the largest pad. This serves as the shave line for the whole foot. Make sure there are no hairs left on or between the toes.
- Shave the face, using a style from the Poodle Heads and Faces section.
- Shave the tail one-third of the length from the base.
- With the #10 blade, shave the abdomen from groin to navel and down the insides of the thighs.
- Shave the anal area (#10 blade), being certain not to put the blade in direct contact with the skin (½" each side).
- With the #10 blade, shave around the neck, one blade width from the base of the ears, base of the skull, and under the jaw. This pattern line should reach to the top of the shoulder on a small dog. (Increase the blade width with the size of the dog, so that the pattern line reaches the top of the shoulder.)
- With the #⅝ blade (for toys/small miniatures) or #10 blade (miniatures/standards), shave a pattern line straight down the center of the back, from the neck pattern to the base of the tail.
- Using the #10 blade (for all sizes of Poodle), shave from the center back pattern down the sides of the abdomen. (This pattern should fall just in front of the rear legs and about 1" behind the front legs.) Continue this pattern around and underneath the abdomen, even with the front pattern line.
- Comb through the coat with the medium comb to remove excess hair.
- Place a cotton ball in each ear (this prevents water from entering the ear canals) and bathe the dog. Fluff dry, using the slicker brush in an upward motion.
- Brush the coat and fluff up, with the wide-toothed comb, all areas to be scissored.
- Using the same blades as before, repeat the process for the pattern, still shaving *with* the lay of the coat and rounding off all pattern corners.
- With the #7 blade, lightly blend down the hair from the pattern. Scissor all straggly hairs from the edges.
- With the wide-toothed comb, fluff up the hair on the chest, between the front legs and underneath, and scissor evenly. (It is acceptable to use the #10 blade on these areas also.)
- Comb the hair on the front legs by the ankles downward and scissor straight around.
- With the wide-toothed comb, fluff up the hair on the front legs and scissor it into straight, tubular shapes. Blend these areas into the body. Scissor evenly the outsides of the legs; continue up and over the shoulders and round off on the tops.
- Comb downward the hair on the rear legs by the ankles and scissor straight around.

158

- With the wide-toothed comb, fluff up the hair on the rear legs and scissor it into straight, full shapes that appear roundish on the hips.
- Scissor the tail into a full round pom-pom.
- Comb the hair on the head straight up and scissor around the edges. Fluff up the hair with the wide-toothed comb and scissor it round on top, tapering it into the ears and neck.
- With the comb, fluff up all of the hair on the legs and front of the body (if the #10 blade was not used) and trim any straggly hairs, especially around the ankles, with the scissors.

The Poodle should be groomed every 4 to 6 weeks, depending on the thickness of the coat and how fast it grows. Regular brushing and combing by the owner, between groomings, will help keep the coat healthy and free of tangles. The ears should be checked weekly and cleaned if necessary, and the toenails should be checked and cut at the grooming session. It should be noted that all shaved areas should be shaved *against* the lay of the coat, except on a dog with sensitive skin. In this case use a #10 blade and shave *with* the lay of the coat. The pattern on the Town and Country clip is shaved with the lay of the coat. DO NOT shave this pattern against the hair grain.

POODLE, CLEAN FACE

Tools and Equipment
Oster A-5 clipper. #10, #15 blades.

Grooming Procedure
- With the #15 blade, fold one ear back and shave from the center of the ear base to the outer corner of the eye. From the outer corner of the eye, shave under the eye to the inner corner and from between the eyes to the tip of the nose. From the lower ear base, shave down to a point at the base of the throat; from the line just made, shave up toward the nose tip and under the lower jaw, pulling the lips back to shave the edges clean.
- Repeat the procedure on the other side of the face.

On a dog with sensitive skin, use the #10 blade on the clipper and shave *with* the lay of the coat, except on the edges of the lips. Otherwise, shave *against* the lay of the coat to achieve a clean, sharp look.

POODLE, MOUSTACHE

Tools and Equipment

Oster A-5 clipper. #10, #15 blades. Scissors. Metal comb (medium).

Grooming Procedure

- With the #15 blade, fold one ear back and shave from the center of the ear base to the outer corner of the eye. From the center of the ear base, shave forward to within ¾" of the corner of the mouth and under the eye to the inner corner. This should create a line from the corner of the mouth to the top of the nose, across and under the chin. From between the eyes, shave down the top of the nose to the tip. From the lower ear base, shave down to a point at the base of the throat; from the line just made, shave up toward the line on the lower jaw.
- Repeat the process on the other side of the face.
- Comb the moustache outward from the nose and chin and scissor the edges evenly.

On a dog with sensitive skin, use the #10 blade on the clipper and shave *with* the lay of the coat.

DONUT MOUSTACHE

Tools and Equipment

Oster A-5 clipper. #10, #15 blades. Scissors. Metal comb (medium).

Grooming Procedure

- With the #15 blade, fold one ear back and shave from the center of the ear base to the outer corner of the eye. From the center of the ear base, shave forward to within ¾" of the corner of the mouth and under the eye to the inner corner of the eye. This creates a line from the corner of the mouth to across the top of the nose and under the chin. From between the eyes, shave to within this line. From the lower ear base, shave down to a point at the base of the throat; from the line just made, shave up toward the line on the lower jaw.
- Repeat the process on the other side of the face.
- Comb the moustache upward and outward, thus making a round donut shape, and scissor the edges evenly.

On a dog with sensitive skin, use the #10 blade on the clipper and shave *with* the lay of the coat.

160

CLEAN FACE

DONUT

CLEAN FACE

MOUSTACHE

FRENCH

POODLE HEADS AND FACES

FRENCH MOUSTACHE

Tools and Equipment

Oster A-5 clipper. #10, #15 blades. Scissors. Metal comb (medium).

Grooming Procedure

- With the #15 blade, fold one ear back and shave from the center of the ear base to the outer corner of the eye. From the center of the ear base, shave forward to within ¾" of the corner of the mouth and under the eye to the inner corner. This should create a line from the corner of the mouth to the top of the nose. From between the eyes, shave down the top of the nose to the tip. From the lower ear base, shave down to a point at the base of the throat; from the line just made, shave up and under the lower jaw, pulling the lips back to shave the edges clean.
- Repeat the process on the other side of the face.
- Comb the moustache straight down and scissor evenly the lower edge.

On a dog with sensitive skin, use the #10 blade on the clipper and shave *with* the lay of the coat, except on the edge of the lips; otherwise, shave *against* the lay of the coat to achieve a clean, sharp look.

PUG

Tools and Equipment

Mink oil spray. Bristle brush. Rubber curry brush. Fine-tooth flea comb. Cotton. Medicated ear powder. Eye drops. Shampoo. After-shampoo skin and coat conditioner. Scissors. Nail clipper. #10 blade. Hound glove. Petroleum jelly. Styptic powder.

Grooming Procedure

- Spray the coat with mink oil and let it remain for 10 to 15 minutes.
- Brush out the coat with a bristle brush or rubber curry brush to loosen any dead hair.
- Comb through the coat with a fine-tooth flea comb.
- Clean under the roll (over the nose) with a damp cotton pad and dry thoroughly.
- Check inside the ears for accumulation of wax or any odor. Clean out the wax with a cotton square and apply ear powder.
- Check the eyes in a good light for anything unusual; Pugs are very susceptible to eye injuries. Clean the eyes with a few eye drops.

- Teeth should be checked for any accumulation of tartar. This can be removed by a veterinarian.
- Remove whiskers on the muzzle with a #10 blade for a nice clean look. (This is usually done on show Pugs.)
- Bathe the dog with a good shampoo. Lightly scrub him, using either your fingers or the curry brush and pay special attention to the legs and under the curl of the tail. With your fingers, clean between the pads of the feet. Rinse and repeat.
- Apply a good skin and coat conditioner and leave it on for 5 minutes. Rinse.
- Either cage or blow dry the dog.
- While the dog is on the grooming table, brush the coat with a bristle brush and comb it with a fine-tooth comb.
- Scissor in an even line the hair on the "pants." Scissor stray hairs on the tail while in its curled position. Scissor any stray hairs on the stomach. When you have finished scissoring, your Pug should have a nice, clean outline.
- Clip the nails very carefully. Pug nails are usually black, so the quick will not be visible; just clip the tips. Have styptic powder on hand just in case you clip a nail too short.
- Apply a small amount of petroleum jelly to the nose.
- Spray the coat with a light mist of coat dressing.
- Finish off by polishing the coat with the hound glove.

Periodically check under the facial roll, particularly if it is a heavy roll. Check the nails every few weeks and do not allow them to grow too long. Check the ears every two weeks.

ROTTWEILER

Tools and Equipment
Nail cutter (scissor or guillotine). Styptic powder. Ear cleaner. Cotton balls. Shampoo (all-purpose or conditioning). Rubber brush. Blending shears. Spray conditioner. Slicker brush.

Grooming Procedure
- Nails should be cut by removing the tips only; avoid cutting the quick. If the nail should bleed, apply styptic powder to stop the bleeding. Any rough nail edges may be smoothed with a file.
- Clean the ears with a liquid cleaner. Apply cleaner to a cotton ball and wipe accumulated dirt and wax from all crevices in both ears.
- With a slicker brush, brush out the entire dog to remove dead coat.
- Bathe the dog in your shampoo of choice and rinse well. A conditioning rinse may be used to help control dandruff. A rubber brush may be used to lather the dog and to remove excess dead coat.
- Towel dry the dog and place him in a cage with a dryer until he is completely dry.
- With blending shears, even up any stray hairs on the back of the thighs, back of the front legs, and the ruff on the neck. Keep trimming to a minimum so as not to be detectable.
- As a final touch, spray a light mist of spray conditioner or coat gloss over the entire dog. With a clean cloth, buff the coat until it shines.

The completed Rottweiler should present a strong, clean outline with a shiny, smooth coat.

SAMOYED

Tools and Equipment
Slicker brush. Mat-splitting comb. Metal rake. Metal comb (wide-tooth). Eye drops (eye stain remover). Shampoo (whitening). Medicated ear powder. Scissors. Toenail clipper. Cotton balls.

Grooming Procedure
- Starting at the head, brush the entire coat with the slicker brush.
- With the metal rake, gently rake through the coat. During the non-shedding season, *do not rake out the undercoat; simply untangle it with the mat-splitting comb and/or metal rake.* Comb through the coat to remove any loosened hair.
- Clean the ears with the medicated ear powder.
- Clean the eyes by wiping with cotton that has been moistened with eye drops. This helps to remove any stains under or around the eyes.
- Cut the tips of the nails with the toenail clipper, being careful not to cut the quick.

With the scissors, snip the whiskers from the muzzle, under the chin, the sides of the face, and above the eyes. (Note: Clipping the whiskers is a decision to be left to the owner, if the dog is not a show dog.)

Place a cotton ball in each ear (this prevents water from entering the ear canals) and bathe the dog. Cage or fluff dry him.

With the scissors, clip the hair between the pads and toes on the feet and around the edges of the feet to give a neat appearance.

Brush and comb through the entire coat.

The Samoyed, because of its white coloring and home environment, should be groomed every 10 to 12 weeks. Regular brushing with a slicker brush, by the owner, will help to keep the coat healthy and the undercoat free of tangles. The ears should be checked weekly and cleaned if necessary, and the toenails should be checked monthly and cut if necessary.

SCOTTISH TERRIER

Tools and Equipment

Slicker brush. Metal comb (medium). Medicated ear powder. Toenail clipper. Eye drops (eye stain remover). Cotton balls. Oster A-5 clipper. #10, #8½, #7, #5 blades. Scissors. Thinning shears.

Grooming Procedure

- Brush the entire coat and tail with the slicker brush. Comb through with the metal comb, paying attention to any tangles.
- Clean the ears, using the medicated ear powder, and lightly pluck any stray hair from the insides.
- Clean the eyes by wiping with cotton that has been moistened with eye drops.
- Cut the tips of the toenails with the toenail clipper, being careful not to cut the quick.
- With the #10 blade on the Oster clipper, shave the anal area, being certain not to put the blade in direct contact with the skin (½" each side).
- Shave the abdomen from groin to navel and down the insides of the thighs.

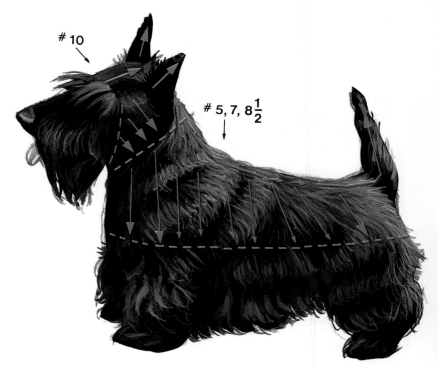

#10

5, 7, 8$\frac{1}{2}$

- With the #10 blade, shave the head, starting at the center of the eyebrows and continuing back to the base of the skull. Again, from the center, shave to the outer corners of the eyes. This line should be about ¾″ above the inner corner of the eye, tapering into the outer corner, thus making a triangle. Next, shave down from the outer corners of the eyes to within ¾″ of the corners of the mouth; continue this line across, under the chin.
- Shave down diagonally from the back edges of the ears to a point at the base of the throat, thus forming a "V" shape.
- There will be a triangular-shaped "tuft" left on the front edge of the ear from halfway along the base on the outside, tapering up to about ¾″ from the tip. Now shave the rest of the ears inside and out.
- With the #8½, #7, or #5 blade (according to the coat length desired, start at the base of the skull and clip down the back to the base of the tail.
- Clip the top half of the tail and blend down either side of the bottom fringe. Comb the fringe downward and scissor the lower edge, making it wide at the base and tapering it to a point at the tip.
- With the clipper, clip down the sides of the neck to the tops of the shoulders.
- Clip down the chest to about 1″ above the breastbone.
- From the first clip down the back, clip down the flanks and hips. (From the side, the pattern should be a straight line from front to back).

167

$^{\#}5, 7, 8\frac{1}{2}$

- Brush and comb through the coat to remove all loosened hair.
- Place a cotton ball in each ear (this prevents water from entering the ear canals) and bathe the dog. Cage dry him.
- Brush and comb through the coat.
- Using the same blade as before, repeat the process for the pattern. With the blade, blend the hair down from the pattern.
- Scissor around the back edges of the ears and the ¾" at the tip on the front edge. Comb the tuft outward and scissor the edge, making it wide at the base and tapering it into the top.
- Comb the eyebrows forward and scissor a "V" in the center for the separation.
- Comb the hair on the face and eyebrows forward and downward, aligning the base of your scissors at the nose and the tip of the scissors at the outer corner of the eye. Scissor the eyebrows from this angle, thus making a deep triangle.
- Lightly scissor stray hairs from around the edges and sides of the beard. Use thinning shears to make the beard appear long and straight.
- With the scissors, snip the hair between the pads of the feet; while the dog is standing, scissor around the edges to give a neat effect.
- Using thinning shears, trim any straggly hairs from the fringes and legs to that they appear even.
- Comb the chest fringe downward and scissor the lower edge straight and even.
- Comb the belly fringe downward and scissor the lower edge evenly, following the contour of the body. Make the belly fringe level with the chest fringe in front and then taper it to the flanks at the rear.
- Lightly comb through the legs, fringes, and face, removing all excess hair.

The Scottish Terrier should be groomed every 6 to 8 weeks. The ears should be checked weekly and cleaned if necessary, and the toenails should be checked and cut at the grooming session.

168

SEALYHAM TERRIER

#5, 7, 8½

#10

Tools and Equipment

Slicker brush. Metal comb. Mat-splitting comb. Toenail clipper. Eye drops (eye stain remover). Medicated ear powder. Oster A-5 clipper. #10, #8½, #7, #5 blades. Scissors. Thinning shears.

Grooming Procedure

- Brush the entire coat and tail with the slicker brush. Comb through with the metal comb and remove any mats or tangles with the mat-splitting comb.
- Clean the ears, using the medicated ear powder, and lightly pluck any stray hair from the insides.
- Clean the eyes by wiping with cotton that has been moistened with eye drops. This will also help to remove any stains.
- Cut the tips of the toenails with the toenail clipper, being careful not to cut the quick.
- With the #10 blade, shave the head, starting at the center of the eyebrows and continuing back to the base of the skull. Again, shave from the center to the outer corners of the eyes. This line should be about ¾" above the inner corner of the eye and should taper into the outer corner, thus forming a triangle. Next shave down from the outer corners of the eyes to within ¾" of the corners of the mouth; continue this line across, under the chin.
- Shave both sides of the ears; from the back edge of the ears, shave down diagonally to a point at the base of the throat, thus forming a "V" shape.

169

- Shave the anal area, being certain not to put the blade in direct contact with the skin (½" each side).
- Shave the abdomen from groin to navel and down the insides of the thighs.
- With the #8½, #7, or #5 blade (according to the coat length desired), start at the base of the skull and clip down the back to the base of the tail.
- With the same blade, clip the entire tail.
- With the clipper, clip down the sides of the neck to the tops of the shoulders.
- Clip down the chest to about one inch above the breastbone.
- From the first clip down the back, clip down the flanks and the hips. (From the side, the pattern should resemble a straight line from front to back.)
- Brush and comb through the coat to remove all excess hair.
- Place a cotton ball in each ear (this prevents water from entering the ear canals) and bathe the dog. Cage or fluff dry.
- Brush and comb through the coat.
- Using the same blade on the Oster A-5 clipper as before, repeat the process for the pattern, blending the hair down from the pattern with the blade.
- Scissor around the edges of the ears.
- Comb the hair on the eyebrows and face forward and downward, aligning the base of your scissors at the nose and the tip of the scissor at the outer corner of the eye. Scissor the eyebrows from this angle, making a triangle. *Make sure that no hair is cut from between the eyebrows or on top of the muzzle.*
- Lightly scissor stray hairs from around the edges and sides of the beard. Use thinning shears to make the beard appear long and straight.
- With scissors, snip the hair between the pads of the feet; while the dog is standing, scissor around the edges to give a neat effect.
- Using thinning shears, trim any straggly hairs from the fringes and legs so that they appear even.
- Comb the chest fringe downward and scissor evenly the ends of the lower edge.
- Comb the belly fringe downward and scissor the ends of the lower edge evenly, following the contour of the body. The belly fringe should be level with the chest fringe in front and taper to the flanks at the rear.
- Lightly comb through the legs, fringes, and face, removing all excess hair.

The Sealyham Terrier should be groomed every 6 to 8 weeks. The ears should be checked weekly, and the toenails should be checked and cut at the grooming session.

Shetland Sheepdog

Tools and Equipment

Slicker brush. Large pin brush. Pure boar bristle brush. Steel comb (fine/medium). Long hair molting comb (#565). Wood utility comb. Scissor. Thinning shear. #10 blade. Ear cleaner. Medicated ear powder. Protein coat conditioner. High velocity dryer. Nail clipper. Tearless protein shampoo. Cotton balls. Oster A-5 clipper.

Grooming Procedure

- Spray the entire coat with protein coat conditioner. This adds body to the coat and helps repair split ends. Brush through the entire coat with a large pin brush, alternating with a slicker brush in matted areas and a molting comb as needed. Work layer by layer, alternating brush and comb to remove mats and loose undercoat. Lift the coat up with your hand, working on thin layers at a time. Brush down and out until all mats and loose hair are removed. Work deeply into the coat, but do not brush to the skin; otherwise, you will cause abrasion. Start at the rear of the dog, at the bottom of the skirt area. Work through the entire coat until the outer coat is separated well and combs smoothly. Work vigorously. The more hair you remove now, the less hair you need to wash and dry.

- Comb through the entire coat with a wide-tooth utility comb. Use a fine-tooth steel comb on the soft hair behind the ears. With your fingers, strip out dead hair behind the ears.
- Swab the ears with a cotton ball that has been moistened with ear cleaner. This will remove dirt and control ear odor. Follow with a dry cotton ball and dust the ears with medicated ear powder.
- Cut the nails with a guillotine-type nail trimmer. Nails should be cut monthly.
- Check between the foot pads and under the feet for burrs, tar, etc. Scissor the hair under the feet even with the pads. Trim any hair around the paw that touches the ground and neaten the entire foot. With thinning shears, trim the hair growing between the toes, which should lie close like a cat's foot.
- Bathe the dog with a tearless protein shampoo that is pH-alkaline. This will add fullness and body to the coat and restructure damaged hair.
- Use a high velocity dryer to blow excess water off the dog while the dog is still in the tub. This will speed up the drying time and help prevent the coat from becoming overly dry. Cage dry the dog until the hair is damp. Then finish drying on the table, using a blow dryer and a pin brush to separate all the hair and remove all of the loose coat.
- Brush the entire coat and be sure to brush to the skin, using the dryer to style and separate the hair. Follow by combing the entire coat.
- The whiskers may be removed with scissors to improve the expression, although this is optional.
- Use a fine comb to finish the head and the ears. Excess hair behind the ears may be thinned with a thinning shear.
- Comb out leg feathering. Trim excess hair on the feet and hocks. The hind legs are to be smooth below the hock joint with a perpendicular line from hock to ground. Leave full the feathering on the forelegs but trim it so that it naturally meets the pastern and does not touch the ground.
- Scissor any long hair under the tail that hangs over the anus. Be sure the anus is clear, and then use a #10 blade to blend down under the tail area so that it does not collect fecal matter.
- Lightly mist the coat with protein coat conditioner to add brilliance and fragrance. Back brush the coat with the pin brush so the coat stands out, away from the body.

SHIH TZU

Tools and Equipment
Slicker brush. Matting comb. Metal combs (medium/fine).
Medicated ear powder. Nail clipper. Eye drops (eye stain remover).
Oster A-5 clipper. #10 blade. Rubber bands. Cotton balls. Scissors.

Grooming Procedure
- Brush the entire coat and tail with the slicker brush, removing any mats with the matting comb. Comb through the coat, using the medium-tooth metal comb.
- Clean the ears, using the medicated ear powder, and lightly pluck stray hair from the insides of the ears.
- Cut the tips of the toenails with the toenail clipper, being careful not to cut the quick.
- Clean the eyes by wiping with cotton that has been moistened with eye drops. Using scissors, snip any stained hair from the corners of the eyes.
- Using a #10 blade, shave the anal area, being certain not to put the blade in direct contact with the skin (½" on either side).
- Using the #10 blade, shave the abdomen from groin to navel and down the insides of the thighs.

173

- Place a cotton ball in each ear (this prevents water from entering the ear canals) and bathe the dog. Fluff dry him.
- Using the medium metal comb, part the coat down the center of the back from the top of the head to the base of the tail. Then make a part from the top of the head to the tip of the nose. An alternating way is to make a part on the head from the outer corner of each eye to the front corner of each ear and across the head from ear to ear. Comb this hair evenly, slightly to the back, and secure it with a rubber band. Attach a bow. Instead, you might want to gather the hair, comb it evenly, and make a braid. Secure the end with a rubber band and attach a bow.
- Scissor the hair between the foot pads. Comb the hair on the legs downward; while the dog is standing, scissor around the edges of the feet to give a round effect.
- Comb through the entire coat with a fine metal comb.

Some dog groomers use cream rinse and similar products on the Shih Tzu; however, I have found, through experience, that these products cause the coat to become more matted in the long run and that a good protein-enriched shampoo is adequate. The longhaired Shih Tzu should be groomed every 2 or 3 weeks. Its ears should be checked weekly, and the nails should be checked at the grooming session.. For owners who prefer a short, cuddly look, use the Teddy Bear clip. See General Information Secion.. For owners who like the longhaired look, even during the heat of the summer, the entire coat can be thinned out so that the dog will be more comfortable. The same instructions apply for grooming, bathing, and fluff drying the Shih Tzu (*i.e.*, steps 1-7).. Part the coat, using the medium metal comb, about 1½" to 2" from the center of the back, down one side. Comb the top hair to the other side (so you do not touch the outer coat), and with thinning shears, thin out the remaining undercoat about 1" at a time. Repeat on the opposite side and across the chest and thighs.. Part the coat down the center of the back and thoroughly comb through it, first with the medium and then with the fine metal comb.. Tie the topknot and scissor the feet, as mentioned before in the grooming instructions for Shih Tzus.

SIBERIAN HUSKY

Tools and Equipment

Slicker brush. Shedding blade. Metal rake. Mat-splitting comb. Eye drops (eye stain remover). Medicated ear powder. Cotton balls. Scissors Toenail clipper. Metal comb (wide-toothed).

Grooming Procedure

- Thoroughly brush the entire coat with the slicker brush. During the shedding season, use the shedding blade (work from the rear to the front). Remove any mats in the undercoat with the mat-splitting comb and the metal rake.
- Clean the ears, using the medicated ear powder, and lightly pluck any stray hair from the insides.
- Clean the eyes by wiping with cotton that has been moistened with eye drops. This will also help to remove stains around the eyes.
- Cut the tips of the toenails with the toenail clipper, being careful not to cut the quick.
- With the scissors, clip the whiskers from the muzzle, chin, sides of the face, and above the eyes. (Note: Clipping the whiskers is a decision to be left to the owner if the dog is not a show dog.)
- Put a cotton ball in each ear (this prevents water from entering the ear canals) and bathe the dog. Cage dry him.
- Brush through the coat briskly with the slicker brush, rake through with the metal rake, and then comb through with the metal comb.
- With the scissors, snip the hair between the pads and toes.

175

SILKY TERRIER

Tools and Equipment

Slicker brush. Metal combs (medium/fine). Medicated ear powder. Nail clipper. Thinning shears. Eye drops (eye stain remover). Oster A-5 clipper. #10 blade. Scissors. Cotton balls.

Grooming Procedure

- Lightly brush the entire coat and tail with the slicker brush, being sure to remove all mats and tangles. Comb through the coat with the medium-tooth metal comb.
- Clean the ears, using the medicated ear powder, and lightly pluck stray hairs from the insides of the ears.
- Cut the tips of the toenails with the toenail clipper, being careful not to cut the quick.
- Clean the eyes by wiping with cotton that has been moistened with eye drops, especially if they are excessively watery and sticky. With scissors snip any stained hair from the corners of the eyes.
- Using a #10 blade, shave the anal area, being certain not to put the blade in direct contact with the skin (½" on either side).
- Using the #10 blade, shave the abdomen from groin to navel and down the insides of the thighs.

176

- Put a cotton ball in each ear (this prevents water from entering the ear canals) and bathe the dog. Fluff dry him.
- Shave the insides of the ears with the #10 blade and, with scissors, snip the long hairs from around the edges of the ears to give a neat appearance.
- With the thinning shears, clip the hair on the back legs from the hock to the foot and to the first joint on the front legs.
- With the scissors, trim any stray hairs on the feet and between the foot pads. While the dog is standing, scissor around the edges of the feet to give a round effect.
- Holding the tail straight out, comb the hair downward on both sides and trim the edge with the scissors to within ½" from the tail.
- Using the medium metal comb, part the coat down the center of the back, from the top of the head to the base of the tail. Then part the hair from the top of the head to the tip of the nose.
- With the fine-tooth metal comb, comb the entire coat downward.

The Silky Terrier should be groomed about every 6 weeks. The ears should be checked weekly (cleaned, if necessary) and the nails should be checked at the grooming session.

SKYE TERRIER

Tools and Equipment
Slicker brush. Matting comb. Metal combs (medium/fine). Medicated ear powder. Nail clipper. Oster A-5 clipper. #10 blade. Cotton balls. Scissors.

Grooming Procedure
- Lightly brush the entire coat and tail with the slicker brush, removing any mats with the matting comb. Comb through the coat with the medium metal comb.
- Clean the ears, using the medicated ear powder, and lightly pluck stray hairs from the insides of the ears.
- Cut the tips of the toenails with the toenail clipper, being careful not to cut the quick.
- Clean the eyes by wiping with cotton that has been moistened with eye drops. With scissors, snip any stained hair from the corners of the eyes.

- Using a #10 blade, shave the anal area, being certain not to put the blade in direct contact with the skin (½″ on either side).
- Using the #10 blade, shave the abdomen from groin to navel and down the insides of the thighs.
- Place a cotton ball in each ear (this prevents water from entering the ear canals) and bathe the dog. Fluff dry him.
- Lightly brush and thoroughly comb through the entire coat with the fine metal comb.
- Using the medium metal comb, part the coat down the center of the back, from the top of the head to the base of the tail. Then make a part from the top of the head to the tip of the nose.
- From the center part, comb all hair downward.
- While the dog is standing, scissor around the outside edges of the feet to give a round effect.
- Holding the tail straight out, comb the hair downward on both sides and scissor the lower edge. Taper the tail to a point. The tail fringe should be as long and full as possible.

Some dog owners use cream rinse and similar products on Silkies; however, I have found, through experience, that these products cause the coat to become more matted in the long run and that a good protein-enriched shampoo is entirely adequate.. The Skye Terrier should be groomed about every 4 weeks. The owner should brush and comb the dog on a regular basis, thus preventing the coat from becoming matted. The ears should be checked weekly and the nails should be checked at the grooming session.

STAFFORDSHIRE BULL

Tools and Equipment
Sisal (natural bristle) brush. Medicated ear powder. Toenail clipper.
Eye drops (eye stain remover). Scissors. Lanolin coat conditioner.
Chamois cloth. Cotton balls.

Grooming Procedure
- Brush the entire coat with the sisal brush, using long deep strokes
  for a thorough massage.
- Clean the ears, using the medicated ear powder.
- Clean the eyes by wiping with cotton that has been moistened with
  eye drops. This will also help to remove stains around the eyes.
- Cut the tips of the toenails with the toenail clipper, being careful not
  to cut the quick.
- With the scissors, snip the whiskers from the muzzle, under the
  chin, the sides of the face, and above the eyes. (Note: Clipping the
  whiskers is a decision to be left to the owner if the dog is not a
  show dog.)

179

- Place a cotton ball in each ear (this prevents water from entering the ear canals) and bathe the dog. Cage dry him.
- Put a few drops of lanolin coat conditioner into the palms of your hands, rub together lightly, and massage this into the coat.
- Brush the coat with the sisal brush to distribute the conditioner, and then lightly rub over the coat with the chamois cloth to give it a nice sheen.

The Staffordshire Bull Terrier should be groomed every 10 to 12 weeks. The ears should be checked weekly and cleaned if necessary, and the toenails should be checked monthly and cut if necessary.

STANDARD SCHNAUZER

Tools and Equipment
Slicker brush. Metal comb (medium). Medicated ear powder. Large toenail clipper. Eye drops (eye stain remover). Cotton balls. Oster A-5 clipper. #10, #8½, #7 blades. Scissors.

Grooming Procedure
- Brush the entire coat with the slicker brush. Comb through with the metal comb.
- Clean the ears, using the medicated ear powder, and lightly pluck any stray hair from the insides.
- Clean the eyes by wiping with cotton that has been moistened with eye drops. This will also help to remove stains around the eyes.
- Cut the tips of the toenails with the toenail clipper, being careful not to cut the quick.
- With the #10 blade, shave the head, starting at the center of the eyebrows and working back to the base of the skull. Then shave from the center again to the outer corners of the eyes. This line should be about ¾" above the inner corner of the eye and should taper into the outer corner, thus making a triangle. Next shave down from the outer corners of the eyes to within ¾" of the corner of the mouth; continue this line across and under the chin.
- Shave both sides of the ears. From the back edges of the ears, shave down diagonally to a point at the base of the throat, thus forming a "V" shape.
- Shave the anal area, being certain not to put the blade in direct contact with the skin (½" on either side).
- Shave the abdomen from groin to navel and down the insides of the thighs.

180

#10

#10, 7, 8$\frac{1}{2}$

- With the #10, #8½, or #7 blade (according to the length of coat desired), start at the base of the skull and clip down the back to the base of the tail.
- Clip the entire tail.
- With the clipper, clip down the sides of the neck to the shoulders and down to the elbows.
- Clip down the chest to the breastbone and slope the pattern down diagonally to the center front of the legs.
- From the first clip down the back, clip down the sides of the abdomen to the flank and from the flank straight down to the hock joint.
- Continue clipping the entire rear end. (From the side view, the pattern line should slope down diagonally from the breastbone, continue straight across the tops of the front legs, slope up across the abdomen and slope down sharply to the hock joint—creating a large "V" on the rear leg.
- Brush through the coat with a slicker brush to remove excess hair.
- Putting a cotton ball in each ear prevents water from entering the ear canals. Bathe the dog and cage dry him.
- Brush and comb through the coat.
- Using the same blade on the Oster A-5 clipper as before, repeat the process for the pattern, blending the hair down on the top of the pattern with the blade.

181

- Scissor around the edges of the ears.
- Scissor a "V" in the center of the eyebrows for the separation.
- Make a part down the center of the muzzle and comb downward. Trim the edges to taper into the outer corners of the eyes.
- Comb the eyebrows forward. Align the base of your scissors with the nose and the tip of your scissor with the outer corner of the eye. Scissor the eyebrows from this angle thus making a deep triangle (being careful not to cut any hair from the top of the muzzle).
- Trim hair between the pads of the feet; while the dog is standing, scissor around the edges to give a round effect. (Doing this first will give you a guide for scissoring the legs.)
- Scissor the front legs into straight tubular shapes.
- Scissor evenly the bottom of the chest fringe.
- Scissor the belly fringe, following the contour of the dog's body and tapering up from the elbows on the front legs to the flanks at the rear.
- Scissor the rear legs, following the natural contours. The insides should be straight to the hock joint and taper up to the shave line.
- Lightly comb through the legs, fringes, and face, removing all excess hair.

The Standard Schnauzer should be groomed every 6 or 8 weeks. The ears should be checked weekly and cleaned if necessary, and the toenails should be checked and cut at the grooming session. *It should be noted that the head, face, and throat should be shaved* with *the grain of the hair.*

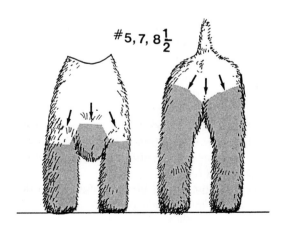

#5, 7, 8½

VIZSLA

Tools and Equipment

Nail cutter (scissor or guillotine). Styptic powder. Ear cleaner.
Cotton balls. Shampoo (all-purpose or conditioning). Stripping
knife. Rubber brush. Blending shears. Straight shears. Spray
conditioner.

Grooming Procedure

- Nails should be cut by removing the tips only; avoid cutting the
  quick. If the nail bleeds, apply styptic powder to stop the bleeding.
  Any rough nail edges may be smoothed by filing.
- Clean the ears with a liquid cleaner. Apply cleaner to a cotton ball
  and wipe accumulated dirt and wax from all crevices in both ears.
- Card (use the stripping knife like a comb) out the coat to remove
  excess hair, if present.
- Bathe the dog in your shampoo of choice. Use a rubber brush to
  lather the dog and to help remove dead coat. Rinse the dog well.
  Apply an after-bath conditioning rinse or use a hot oil treatment if
  the dog has dandruff.
- Towel dry the dog and place him in a cage with a dryer until he is
  completely dry.
- Any seams (where two different growths of hair come together)
  may be blended. Excess hair on the back of the thigh may be
  removed, as well as untidy hair on the back edge of the front legs.
  The underneath side of the tail may be neatened up too.
- Whiskers and eyebrows may be removed if desired.

183

Weimaraner

Tools and Equipment

Nail clipper (scissor or guillotine). Styptic powder. Ear cleaner. Cotton balls. Shampoo (all-purpose or conditioning). Stripping knife. Rubber brush. Blending shears. Straight shears. Spray conditioner.

Grooming Procedure

- Nails should be cut by removing the tips only. Avoid cutting the quick, although if a nail bleeds, apply styptic powder to stop the bleeding. Any rough nail edges may be smoothed with a file.
- Clean the ears with a liquid ear cleaner. Apply ear cleaner to a cotton ball and wipe accumulated wax and dirt from all crevices in both ears.
- Card (use stripping knife like a comb) out the coat to remove excess hair, if present.
- Bathe the dog in your shampoo of choice. Use a rubber brush to lather the dog and to help remove dead coat. Rinse the dog well.

184

Apply an after-bath conditioning rinse or use a hot oil treatment if the dog has dandruff.

- Towel dry the dog and place him in a cage with a dryer until he is completely dry.
- Any seams (where two different directions of hair growth come together) may be blended. Excess hair on the back of the thighs may be removed, as well as untidy hair on the back of the front legs. The underneath side of the tail may be neatened up, too.
- Whiskers and eyebrows may be removed if desired.
- As a final touch, lightly apply a small amount of spray conditioner or coat gloss to the coat and buff with a clean cloth or a hound brush until shiny.

The completed Weimaraner should have a crisp outline and a shiny coat. This grooming should be done every 10 to 12 weeks.

WELSH TERRIER

Tools and Equipment
Slicker brush. Metal comb (medium). Medicated ear powder. Toenail clipper. Eye drops (eye stain remover). Cotton balls. Oster A-5 clipper. #10, #8½, #7, #5 blades. Scissors. Thinning shears.

Grooming Procedure
- Brush the entire coat and tail with the slicker brush. Comb through with the metal comb, paying attention to any tangles.
- Clean the eyes by wiping with cotton that has been moistened with eye drops. This will also help to remove stains around the eyes.
- Clean the ears, using the medicated ear powder, and lightly pluck any stray hair from the insides.
- Cut the nails with a guillotine-type nail trimmer. Nails should be cut monthly.
- With the #10 blade, shave the head, starting at the center of the eyebrows and continuing back to the base of the skull. Then shave from the center again to the outer corners of the eyes. This line should be about ¾" above the inner corner of the eye, tapering into the outer corner to create a triangle. Next, shave down from the outer corners of the eyes to within ¾" from the corners of the mouth and continue this line across, under the chin.
- Shave both sides of the ears; from the back edge of the ears, shave down diagonally to a point at the base of the throat, thus forming a "V" shape.

- Shave the anal area, being certain not to put the blade in direct contact with the skin (½" on either side).
- Shave the abdomen from groin to navel and down the insides of the thighs.
- With the #8½, #7, or #5 blade (according to the length of coat desired), start at the base of the skull and clip down the back to the base of the tail.
- Clip the top half of the tail and blend down either side of the fringe. Comb the fringe downward and scissor the lower edge, thus making a feather shape.
- With the clipper, clip down the sides of the neck to the shoulder and down to the elbow.
- Clip down the chest to the breastbone and slope the pattern down diagonally to the cente rfront of the legs.
- From the first clip down the back, clip down the sides of the abdomen, arching the pattern over the hips. (From the side, the pattern line should slope down diagonally from the breastbone, continue straight across the tops of the front legs, slope up across the abdomen, and arch up over the hips and down to a point in the rear.)
- Brush through the coat with the slicker brush to remove any excess hair.
- Place a cotton ball in each ear (this prevents water from entering the ear canals) and bathe the dog. Cage dry him.
- Brush and comb through the coat.
- Using the same blade on the Oster A-5 clipper as before, repeat the process for the pattern, blending the hair down from the top of the pattern with the blade.
- Scissor around the edges of the ears.
- Scissor a "V" in the center of the eyebrows.
- Comb the hair on the face and eyebrows forward and downward, aligning the base of your scissors with the nose and pointing the tip of the scissors toward the outer corner of the eye. Scissor the eyebrows from this angle, thus making a deep triangle. Be careful not to cut any hair from the top of the muzzle.
- Lightly scissor stray hairs from around the edge and sides of the beard. Use thinning shears to shape the beard, which should be long and barrel-shaped.
- Use thinning shears to trim any stray hairs from the top of the muzzle.
- Trim hair between the pads of the feet; while the dog is standing, scissor around the edges to give a round effect. Doing this first will give you a guide for scissoring the legs.
- Scissor the front legs into straight tubular shapes.
- Scissor evenly the bottom of the chest fringe.

186

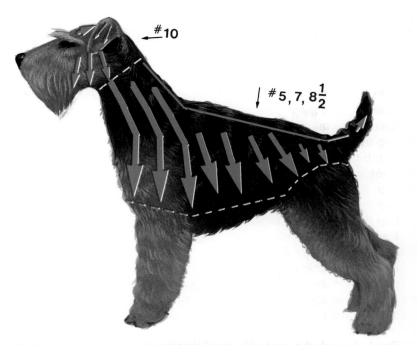

#10

$\downarrow$ #5, 7, 8$\frac{1}{2}$

- Scissor the bottom of the belly fringe, following the contour of the dog's body and tapering up from the elbows on the front legs to the flanks at the rear.
- Scissor the rear legs, following the natural contours. (From the back view, the legs should be straight on the outsides. Inside, they should be straight, up to the thighs, and then arch up and into the shave line.)
- Lightly comb through the legs, fringes, and face, removing all excess hair and trimming any stray hairs as necessary.

The Welsh Terrier should be groomed every 6 or 8 weeks. The ears should be checked weekly and cleaned if necessary, and the toenails should be checked and cut at the grooming session. It should be noted that the head, face, and throat should be shaved *with* the grain of the hair.

#5, 7, 8$\frac{1}{2}$, 10

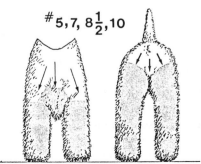

WEST HIGHLAND WHITE

#5, 7, 8½

Tools and Equipment
Mineral oil. Cotton balls. Alcohol. Styptic powder. Nail clipper.
Slicker brush. Comb. Oster A-5 clipper. #10, #8½, #7, #5 blades.
Scissors. Thinning shears.

Grooming Procedure
- Trim the tips of the nails with the nail clipper. Have styptic powder handy in case the vein inside the nail bleeds. You might prefer to do this in the tub; dogs are less nervous there.
- Brush through the coat with a slicker brush, removing all mats, tangles, dead hair, and other debris.
- The ears can be cleaned with cotton and liquid ear cleaner; however, it is recommended that you use alcohol in place of the cleaner.
- Using your Oster A-5 clipper and #10 blade, clip within one-half inch on either side of the anus.

188

- With the same blade, remove all hair from the groin area.
- Using the same clipper with a #5, #7, or #8½ blade (depending on coat length preference), clip from the top of the neck down to the base of the tail.
- From the top of the neck, clip down to the shoulders.
- Using the shoulders as a guide line, clip down the body to the rump in the same fashion.
- With the same blade, clip from the top of the neck down to the breastbone.
- With the #10 blade, clip the top half of the ear.
- With your scissors, round off the top of the ears to give a neat appearance.
- Using the same blade, clip from the base to the tip of the tail, leaving the hair on the opposite side.
- Using your thinning shears, trim the hair on the other side of the tail in the shape of half a Christmas tree (leave the base of the tail longer).
- Trim the hair under the feet so that it is even with the foot pads.
- Using your scissors, trim the hair on the bottom of the feet to give a round appearance.
- Use thinning shears on the Westie's head, making the front view of the face look round.
- The eyebrows may be trimmed with thinning shears to create an awning shape from the side. There should be only one long eyebrow, which resembles a visor.
- Carefully trim the hair from under the eyes.
- Bathe the dog. Because the Westie is a white-haired dog, you may want to use whitening shampoo or shampoo for sensitive skin.
- Cage or fluff dry.
- Comb out the dog, and use your thinning shears to trim away any fly-away hairs that are out of place.

The Westie should be groomed every 4 to 6 weeks.

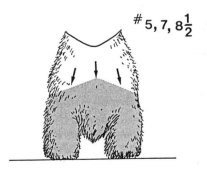

$$^\# 5, 7, 8\tfrac{1}{2}$$

YORKSHIRE TERRIER

Tools and Equipment
  Slicker brush. Matting comb. Metal combs (medium/fine).
  Medicated ear powder. Nail clipper. Eye drops (eye stain remover).
  Oster A-5 clipper. #15, #10 blades. Rubber bands. Cotton balls.
  Scissors.

Grooming Procedure
- Brush the entire coat with the slicker brush. The coats vary on these
  dogs, from fine and silky to thick and cottonlike. The latter tends to
  mat easily; if this should happen, use a small matting comb to
  remove the mats. Finish all dogs (whether silky or cottony textured)
  by combing through the coat with the fine metal comb.
- Clean the ears, using the medicated ear powder, and lightly pluck
  stray hair from the insides of the ears.
- Cut the tips of the toenails with the toenail clipper, being careful not
  to cut the quick.
190

- Clean the eyes by wiping with cotton that has been moistened with eye drops. If the eyes are excessively watery and sticky, with scissors, snip stained hair from the corners.
- Using a #15 blade, shave the tips of the ears (approximately ½") inside and out. Scissor the hair around the shaved tips for a neat finish.
- Using the #10 blade, shave the anal area, being certain not to put the blade in direct contact with the skin (½" on either side).
- Using the #10 blade, shave the abdomen from groin to navel and down the insides of the thighs.
- Place a cotton ball in each ear (this prevents water from entering the ear canals) and bathe the dog. Fluff dry him.
- With the medium metal comb, part the coat down the center of the back from the top of the head to the base of the tail.
- Make a part on the head from the outer corner of each eye to the front corner of each ear and across the head from ear to ear. Comb this hair evenly, slightly to the back, and secure it with a rubber band. Attach a bow. An alternative is to gather the hair, comb it evenly, and make a small braid. Secure the end with a rubber band and then the bow.
- Scissor the hair between the foot pads. Comb the hair on the legs downward; while the dog is standing, scissor around the edges of the feet to give a round effect.
- Scissor the hair underneath the tail and round the edges of the tail for a neat appearance.
- Comb through the entire coat with a fine-tooth metal comb.

Some dog groomers use cream rinse and similar products on the Yorkie; however, I have found, through experience, that these products cause the coat to become more matted in the long run, and that a good protein-enriched shampoo is entirely adequate.. The long-coated Yorkshire Terrier should be groomed every 3 or 4 weeks. The ears should be checked weekly, and the nails should be checked at the grooming session.. An alternative, for owners who prefer a short, cuddly look, is the Teddy Bear clip.

INDEX

Affenpinscher, 49
Afghan Hound, 51
Airedale Terrier, 52
Akita, 55
Alaskan Malamute, 57
Anal pore, 26
Australian Terrier, 58
Basset Hound, 60
Bathing, 12
Beagle, 62
Bearded Collie, 63
Bedlington Terrier, 65
Blow drying, 13-14
Border Terrier, 68
Borzoi, 70
Boston Terrier, 71
Bouvier des Flandres, 72
Boxer, 75
Brittany Spaniel, 76
Brush burns, 29
Bulldog, 78
Cardigan Welsh Corgi, 79
Chesapeake Bay
   Retriever, 43
Chewing, 26-27
Chihuahua (long coat), 43
Chow Chow, 84
Clipping, 30
Clumber Spaniel, 87
Coat, conditioning the, 19
Cockapoo, 28
Cocker Spaniel,
   American, 86
Cocker Spaniel, English,
   88
Collie, rough coat, 90
Collie, smooth coat, 92
Colognes, 27
Combs, 34
Corded Coat, 17
Curly-coated Retriever, 95
Dachshund, long coat, 94
Dachshund, smooth coat,
   95
Dachshund, wire coat, 96
Dalmatian, 97
Dematting, 11
Deodorizers, 15
Diet, 12
Doberman Pinscher, 98
Dry cleaners, 20

Ears, cleaning the, 16
English Setter, 99
English Springer Spaniel,
   101
Equipment, 30
Eyes, cleaning the, 18
Feet, grooming the, 24
Flat-coated Retriever, 103
Forced drying, 22
Fox Terrier, smooth, 105
Fox Terrier, wire, 106
French Bulldog, 109
German Shepherd Dog,
   110
German Shorthaired
   Pointer, 111
German Wirehaired
   Pointer, 112
Golden Retriever, 114
Great Dane, 115
Greyhound, 116
Grooming post, 37
Gumabone®, 43
Handling, 29
Hound glove, 33
Hydraulic tables, 36
Irish Setter, 118
Italian Greyhound, 121
Keeshond, 122
Kerry Blue Terrier, 124
Labrador Retriever, 127
Lather machine, 40
Lhasa Apso, 128
Miniature Schnauzer, 132
Mixed breed, 47
Nail clippers, 36
Nail clipping, 19
Newfoundland, 134
Norwegian Elkhound, 135
Nylabone®, 43
Odors, doggie, 27
Old English Sheepdog,
   137
Oster clippers, 40
Pekingese, 138
Pembroke Welsh Corgi,
   140
Plucking, 28
Pointer, 141
Pomeranian, 142
Poodle (Dutch clip), 146

Poodle Heads and Faces,
   Clean face, 159
Poodle Head and Faces,
   French Moustache, 196
Poodle Heads and Faces,
   161
   Moustache, 197-198
Poodle (Kennel clip), 144
Poodle (Lamb clip), 149
Poodle (Puppy clip), 151
Poodle (Royal Dutch clip),
   153
Poodle (Summer clip),
   155
Poodle (Town and
   Country clip), 157
Pug, 162
Ramp, 40
Rottweiler, 164
Samoyed, 165
Schnoodle, 28
Scissors and shears, 19-
   20, 25
Scissoring, 17
Scottish Terrier, 166
Sealyham Terrier, 169
Shar-pei, 18. See also
   Chinese Shar-pei
Shedding, 28
Shetland Sheepdog, 171
Shih Tzu, 173
Siberian Husky, 175
Silky Terrier, 176
Skye Terrier, 177
Staffordshire Bull Terrier,
   179
Standard Schnauzer, 180
Stripping, 28
Stripping knife, 49
"Teddy Bear" clip, 46
Vizsla, 183
Weimaraner, 184
Welsh Terrier, 185
West Highland White
   Terrier, 188
Whiskers, removing the,
   27
Wrinkles, cleaning facial,
   18
Yorkshire Terrier, 190